CREATIVE CAN-DO CRAFTS

Boost Kids' Confidence as You Build Their Faith

By Lois Keffer

Loveland, Colorado

"The Lord your God will bless you in all your harvest and in all the work of your hands, and your joy will be complete" (Deuteronomy 16:15, NIV).

With warmest thanks to Tim Botts and Jeanne Downing, and to the memory of Albert Affeld—three master teachers whose incredible gifts of art and music have brought beauty into my life, and allowed me to pass that beauty on to others.

CREATIVE CAN-DO CRAFTS

Copyright © 1997 Lois Keffer

Credits
Editors: Jody Brolsma and Jan Kershner
Creative Development Editor: Paul Woods
Chief Creative Officer: Joani Schultz
Copy Editor: Helen Turnbull
Art Director: Lisa Chandler
Assistant Art Director: Kari K. Monson
Cover Art Director: Helen H. Lannis
Computer Graphic Artist: Ray Tollison
Cover Designer: Diana Walters
Illustrators: Megan Jeffrey, Lois Keffer, and Ray Tollison
Production Manager: Ann Marie Gordon

Unless otherwise noted, Scriptures quoted from The Youth Bible, New Century Version, copyright © 1991 by Word Publishing, Dallas, Texas 75039. Used by permission.

Library of Congress Cataloging-in-Publication Data
Keffer, Lois.
    Creative can-do crafts : boost kids' confidence as you build their
faith / by Lois Keffer.
        p. cm.
    Includes index.
    ISBN 1-55945-682-5
    1. Christian education—Activity programs. 2. Creative activities
and seat work. 3. Christian education of children. I. Title.
    BV1536.K38 1997
    268'.432—dc21   97-2346
10 9 8 7 6 5 4 3   06 05 04 03 02 01 00 99 98   CIP
Printed in the United States of America.

CONTENTS

BEAUTEMOUS BOTANICALS 68

PAPER CAPERS 83

INSTANT HOLIDAY HELPERS 95

SCRIPTURE INDEX 109

INTRODUCTION

IN THE BEGINNING, God *created* the heavens and the earth. On the sixth day, God created people in his image. There you have the origin of the creative drive in each of us—we're made in the image of our Creator—God.

But our need for self-expression comes out in very different ways. See if this sounds familiar: You set out colored pencils and paper and invite kids to draw whatever comes to mind. Some kids draw crooked houses and stick-figure people, some scribble out bold, abstract designs and say, "I'm finished" in thirty seconds. Some create thoughtful, charming flower compositions that will stay on refrigerators for a year, and some use the pencils as drumsticks to beat out jarring rhythms on tables or on their neighbors' heads!

All of the above responses make important statements about the kids who produced them. The crooked houses and stick-figure drawings say, "This is how I see my world. It's fun and colorful and bright, and I'm not too worried about the details." The bold, abstract, thirty-second masterpieces say, "Bright colors and big motions are cool but the rest of this is for wimps, and I don't have time for it." The charming flower compositions say, "I'm highly visual and my small-motor skills are so well-developed that I could do this all day." The drumstick dropouts are saying, "My large muscles have gotta move right now! I can't sit still for anything or anybody. There's gotta be a way to have fun here."

CAN ALL THESE KIDS ENJOY CRAFT TIME? You bet! How? With projects that appeal to diverse needs and skill levels. Please read on.

In your mind, put Annabella Artist at a table filled with paper doilies, heart stickers, glitter, lace, netting, glue, and little curlicues of potpourri. In fifteen minutes she'll produce a valentine that would make the artists at Hallmark weep.

Now set All-Thumbs Arlo across from Annabella. Arlo makes a dubious-looking pile of doilies and lace, dumps glitter on top of it, glues the whole thing to three fingers of his left hand, then rubs glitter in his eyes. Through the painful haze he sees the teacher cooing over Annabella's masterpiece. Aargh—foiled again!

Multiply this experience by the number of craft projects Arlo will have to endure as he toils down the road to manhood. It's not a pretty sight. Is Arlo doomed to discouragement and humiliation every time scissors and glue appear? No!

WHILE NOT ALL KIDS ARE CAPABLE OF TURNING OUT MASTER-PIECES, all kids *do* have God-given creativity, and the projects in this book will help them express it.

Art for kids needs to focus on the process, not just the product. Put a hammer in Arlo's hand and watch his large muscle groups respond as he happily pounds and punches. See his delight meter go over the top as he stomps through slimy paint, models with gloppy goo, and devours a sculpture made from delicious dough.

Creative Can-Do Crafts provides you with a wide range of projects that appeal to kids of all sizes, ages, and abilities. You'll find everything from simple paper crafts to zany tie-dyes, from edible dirt soufflés to zooming balloon rockets. Kids will be delighted with the variety you offer them and anxious to see what you'll come up with next!

ALL THE NEEDED SUPPLIES ARE READILY AVAILABLE at discount, hardware, or craft stores. So when you've chosen a craft, you can be up and running with it in no time. The clear, step-by-step instructions and illustrations will lead you easily through each project. It's always a great idea to make a sample craft ahead of time so you feel confident and comfortable with the process and can explain it easily to your kids.

Along with the crafts, you'll find Scriptures and Faith Boosters that transform craft time into a time for spiritual growth. You'll lead kids in a variety of activities that use the finished crafts (or some element involved in making them) to teach an important spiritual truth. The finished craft projects will remind kids of what they've learned. And when kids share their crafts and their knowledge with others, you'll know that you've done a lot more than just fill time with an art project!

At the end of the book you'll find Instant Holiday Helpers. These patterns for 3-D seasonal paper crafts are a craft leader's lifesaver. All you need is a photocopier, paper, scissors, markers, glue, and tape, and you're ready for your kids to create all kinds of seasonal delights. So when you're caught in pinch, just photocopy and go!

As you explore the projects in *Creative Can-Do Crafts* with your kids, these tips will help you make craft time a great time for everyone.

● **ALLOW FOR PERSONAL** choice in projects, colors, and materials. When kids have the freedom of choice, you'll find them willing to invest themselves in their work.

● **CONSIDER WHAT KINDS OF LEARNERS YOU HAVE,** and set your expectations accordingly. *Expect* kinesthetic learners to need to use those large muscle groups. *Expect* nonvisual learners to finish quickly and want to move on to something else.

● **FREE KIDS** from the stress and frustration of trying to emulate a perfect sample craft made by an artistic adult.

● **USE MUSIC** to set a mood appropriate to the project. Quiet, peaceful worship songs will encourage kids to work thoughtfully. Happy, upbeat kids' songs will produce enthusiasm and the use of lots of bright colors.

● **AVOID TRUMPED-UP PRAISE.** Instead, offer realistic, encouraging comments, such as "Tell me about what you're doing," or "I'm interested to see where you're going with this."

● **BY YOUR ENCOURAGING ATTITUDE,** show kids that good fun is as important as good art.

You can make craft time a positive, fulfilling time for everyone if you bear in mind that your number one job is to help kids become the people God made them to be.

Happy crafting!

Lois Keffer

"May the favor of the Lord our God rest upon us; establish the work of our hands for us—yes, establish the work of our hands" (Psalm 90:17, New International Version).

THE WELL-STOCKED CRAFT CUPBOARD

These are items commonly used in *Creative Can-Do Crafts* that you'll want to hoard, beg for, or purchase.

CRAFT SUPPLIES	HOUSEHOLD ITEMS	NATURE ITEMS
lightweight jute twine	waxed paper	twigs
tacky glue	margarine tubs	pressed flowers
hot glue gun	whipped-topping tubs	pressed leaves
glue sticks	mixing bowls	Spanish moss
acrylic craft paint	plastic spoons	pine cones
paint brushes	plastic knives	
scissors	baby-food jars	
permanent markers	fabric scraps	
yarn	buttons	
clean cardboard	newspaper	
poster board	cookie sheets	
unbleached muslin	paper grocery bags	
pencils		

POUND, PUNCH, AND BUILD

SMOKING VOLCANOES

"Mount Sinai was covered with smoke, because the Lord came down on it in fire. The smoke rose from the mountain like smoke from a furnace, and the whole mountain shook wildly" (Exodus 19:18).

● ●

Baking soda and vinegar provide an impressive "poof" for this great craft.

1. Form trios. Give each trio three small paper plates, three baby-food jars, and a mixing bowl.

2. Have each trio put two cups of salt, one cup of flour, and seven-eighths cup of water in the mixing bowl. Let kids take turns mixing and kneading the dough until it becomes firm and holds its shape easily.

3. Place a baby-food jar in the center of a paper plate. Demonstrate how to build a dough "volcano" with the jar as its crater. Have trios divide their dough into three parts, then instruct each child to build a volcano.

4. As children finish their volcanoes, pass around a box of baking soda. Have each child put a teaspoon of the soda into his or her jar.

5. Tint three different containers of vinegar with red, yellow, and blue food coloring. Let kids each choose a color, then pour one-third cup of vinegar into their volcanoes. Be sure to applaud as the volcanoes "erupt" with colored foam.

FAITH BOOSTER

Dim the room and shine flashlights on the volcanoes as they erupt.
Read Exodus 19:16-19. Ask:

● **What would it be like to see smoke, fire, and lightning and to hear thunder coming from the top of a mountain?**

● **What do you think God was trying to teach the Israelites with the smoke and fire?**

Explain that God used many miraculous signs to remind the Israelites that he was in charge and that they should worship and obey him. Mention the plagues in Egypt, the opening of the Red Sea, the cloud and pillar of fire, and the provision of food in the wilderness. Ask:

● **What reminds us of God's greatness and power today?**

● **What helps you remember to obey God?**

SUPPLIES

❑ small paper plates
❑ salt
❑ flour
❑ water
❑ mixing bowls
❑ baby-food jars
❑ food coloring
❑ vinegar
❑ baking soda
❑ teaspoons

PRO POINTER

If the salt dough is soft and sticky, add a bit more flour and salt. If it's too grainy, add a little water.

BALLOON ROCKETS

"You make the winds your messengers, and flames of fire are your servants" (Psalm 104:4).

SUPPLIES

- ❑ balloons
- ❑ straws
- ❑ string
- ❑ tape

This entertaining, reusable craft will blow kids away!

1. Form pairs. Give each pair two balloons, two four-foot lengths of string, two straws, and four two-inch strips of tape.
2. Show kids how to slip their strings through their straws.
3. Have one partner blow up his or her balloon and pinch the opening. Let the other partner use two pieces of tape to connect the inflated balloon to a straw.
4. Have each partner grasp one end of the string and pull it taut. When the partner with the inflated balloon lets it go, the "rocket" will fly along the string.
5. Repeat with the other partner's balloon.

FAITH BOOSTER

Ask:

● **What kind of power do your rockets use?**

Tell kids you're going to see how much wind power they can produce. Form two lines facing each other, five feet apart. Place cotton balls on the floor in front of each child in one line. Have the kids in that line blow the cotton balls to the other line and then scoot back to their starting places. Let kids in the other line blow the cotton balls back to the first line. As kids catch their breath, read Psalm 104:1-8 aloud. Ask:

● **How many people do you think it would take to blow the shoreline of the ocean back a mile or so? a half-mile? a hundred yards?**

● **How many people would it take to blow a storm cloud back where it came from?**

● **How does it feel to know that our God can *easily* do those things?**

Close with a simple prayer praising God for his awesome power.

TiN-CAN VOTiVE CANDLEHOLDERS

"Later, Jesus talked to the people again, saying, 'I am the light of the world. The person who follows me will never live in darkness but will have the light that gives life'" (John 8:12).

●　●

These simple or fancy-as-you-please candleholders are whackin' good fun to make, and they glow with flickering patterns of light when you add votive candles.

1. Rinse and remove labels from empty tin cans—any size can is OK. Be sure to file any sharp edges. Fill cans with water to within a half-inch of the tops and place them in a freezer overnight.

2. Form pairs and give each pair a permanent marker, a hammer, a nail, a stack of newspapers, and two of the frozen cans. Encourage kids to hold their cans with several thicknesses of newspaper to protect their fingers from the cold.

3. Have kids use permanent markers to draw designs with a series of dots at least a half-inch apart. Kids might draw designs such as hearts, crosses, their initials, or wavy lines.

4. Have one partner hold a can (with several thicknesses of newspaper) as the other partner punches out a design by placing a nail on each dot and tapping *lightly*. It doesn't take much force to punch through the frozen can, so encourage kids to start with very light taps and strike harder as needed.

5. When kids have finished punching out their designs, have them set their cans in a sink filled with warm water. When the ice falls out, let kids dry the cans and drop in a votive candle.

SUPPLIES

- ❏ empty tin cans
- ❏ metal file
- ❏ water
- ❏ permanent markers
- ❏ hammers
- ❏ nails
- ❏ newspaper
- ❏ votive candles or tea lights
- ❏ long matches

FAiTH BOOSTER

Set all the finished candleholders on a table in the center of a darkened room. Light a long match, and read John 8:12 by its light. Then let kids come to the table one by one and light their candles with assistance from an adult. As kids light their candles, have the other kids say, "Jesus is the light of the world for (name of child)." When each child has lit his or her candle and received affirmation, ask:

- **How is Jesus a light in your life?**
- **How can you share Jesus' light with others?**

Close with a prayer thanking Jesus for the light he brings to our lives.

TIN-PUNCH PIE PANS

"'Isn't my message like a fire?' says the Lord. 'Isn't it like a hammer that smashes a rock?'" (Jeremiah 23:29).

● ●

SUPPLIES

- ❑ *aluminum pie pans*
- ❑ *pencils*
- ❑ *newspaper*
- ❑ *permanent markers*
- ❑ *nails*
- ❑ *hammers*
- ❑ *jute twine*
- ❑ *optional: eyelet or ribbon edging, hot glue gun, needle-nose pliers*

The old-world art of tin punch is remarkably easy and rewarding for elementary kids. A great gift idea!

1. Give each child a pie pan, a marker, and a thick stack of newspapers. Let kids trace onto newspaper the smaller circles that form the bottom of their pie pans. Have them pencil dot-designs that fit within the circles, then use permanent markers to redraw the designs on the inside of their pie pans.

Or give kids photocopies of the "God Is Love" pattern (p. 13). Allow each child to poke through the dots with a sharp pencil, place the pattern in the pie pan, and mark each dot with a permanent marker.

2. Form pairs and instruct kids to place their pie pans facing up on top of their stacks of newspaper on the floor. Have one partner hold a pie pan while the other partner uses a hammer and nail to punch a hole through each dot.

3. Demonstrate how to punch two small holes near the top of the pie pan, thread a length of jute twine through the holes, and tie the twine to form a hanger.

FAITH BOOSTER

Let kids each choose a small rock and then take turns striking their rocks with a hammer to see if the rocks will chip or break. Have kids wear safety goggles as they strike the rocks, and make sure observers are standing several feet back. After everyone has had a turn, talk about how easy it was to punch through a pie pan, but how few rocks (if any) broke. Ask:

● **How is the Bible like a hammer so powerful that it could break rocks?**

● **How can you tell the Bible is powerful in your life?**

Close with a brief prayer thanking God for the power of his Word.

PRO POINTER

Kids may wish to add an eyelet or ribbon edging. As an adult operates a hot glue gun, let kids use needle-nose pliers to put the edging in place.

CD HOLDERS

"Shout with joy to the Lord, all the earth; burst into songs and make music" (Psalm 98:4).

● ●

SUPPLIES

- ❏ *six-inch pieces of one-by-six-inch pine*
- ❏ *medium and fine-grain sandpaper*
- ❏ *sanding blocks or wood scraps*
- ❏ *tack cloth*
- ❏ *electric drill and three-inch boring bit*
- ❏ *twelve-inch pieces of one-half-inch dowel*
- ❏ *wood stain*
- ❏ *disposable pie pans*
- ❏ *small, disposable foam brushes*
- ❏ *rags*
- ❏ *paint thinner*
- ❏ *newspaper*
- ❏ *paper towels*
- ❏ *wood glue*

This handsome CD holder—which also holds cassettes—makes a great addition to any child's room or a gift kids would be proud to give.

Plan to do this project outside to simplify cleanup.

1. Have an adult drill three one-half-inch holes in each section of pine as shown in the diagram on page 15.

2. Give each child two six-inch lengths of one-by-six-inch pine, three twelve-inch lengths of dowel, and a piece of medium or fine-grain sandpaper attached to a sanding block or scrap of wood. Have kids spread out newspaper, sand all edges and surfaces, then wipe them with a tack cloth.

3. Pour small amounts of wood stain into disposable pie pans. Help kids use foam brushes to stain their wood pieces and dowels. Demonstrate how to rub and wipe the stain with rags to achieve a smooth finish.

4. Help kids insert the dowels into the holes in the wood pieces. If the dowels don't fit snugly into the holes, spread a few drops of wood glue on the inside of each hole. Set the finished holders in a warm, sunny place to dry.

5. Have an adult help clean the stain from kids' hands with paint thinner and paper towels.

FAITH BOOSTER

Before this session, record on a cassette fifteen-second segments of several different kinds of music. Have kids sit on the floor with their arms wrapped around their knees, and their heads down. Have them listen to the music you've recorded. After each segment, pause the tape and ask questions such as "How does that music make you feel?" or "What does that music make you feel like doing?" Explain that music can affect our hearts as well as our minds. Read Psalm 98:4 aloud, then ask:

- ● **How do you choose the music you listen to?**
- ● **What kind of music is pleasing to God?**

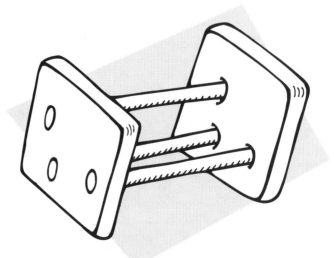

TWIG FRAMES

"Remain in me, and I will remain in you. A branch cannot produce fruit alone but must remain in the vine. In the same way, you cannot produce fruit alone but must remain in me" (John 15:4).

SUPPLIES

❑ *sturdy cardboard or poster board*
❑ *utility or craft knife*
❑ *grocery bags*
❑ *twigs*
❑ *hot glue gun or craft glue*
❑ *Spanish moss*
❑ *double-sided tape*
❑ *photocopies of John 15:4*

PRO POINTER

Here's another great twig craft. Have kids glue twigs vertically around baby-food jars or small cans, wrap the twigs twice with jute twine, and tie the twine in a bow. Voilà—you have great looking vases!

Half the fun of this great craft is in the gathering! Plan to take your kids on a mini-hike to a wooded area to gather twigs. Remind them not to disturb wildflowers or animal homes.

1. Before craft time, use a utility or craft knife to cut two eight-by-ten-inch pieces of cardboard or poster board for each child. From half of the cardboard pieces, cut a five-by-seven-inch rectangle from the center to create frames. The solid pieces will serve as backing for the frames.

2. Distribute photocopies of John 15:4.

3. Hand out grocery bags, and let children collect twigs in a wooded area. Have kids select twelve to fifteen twigs of about the same thickness. The twigs should be eight to ten inches long. Kids may also collect other small "nature treasures" such as tiny pine cones, seeds, and feathers.

4. When you've returned to your classroom, give each child two prepared cardboard pieces, one front piece and one backing piece. Have children arrange their twigs and other nature items around the opening of the frames.

5. Once kids are satisfied with the arrangement of their twigs, let them use craft glue to affix the twigs to the cardboard frames. Or, have an adult helper use a hot glue gun to attach the twigs according to kids' directions. Have kids poke bits of Spanish moss between the twigs where the cardboard shows through.

6. While the twig frames dry, have kids attach double-sided tape to three sides of the backing pieces. Help kids carefully center the verses on the backing pieces and then lay the frames on top of the backing pieces and press them together. Remind kids to keep their frames flat until the glue has dried.

FAITH BOOSTER

Have kids sit in a circle. Hold up three or four leftover twigs. Ask:
● **Will this twig ever grow? What about this one? Or this one?**
● **Why won't these twigs grow?**
Read John 15:4 aloud. Ask:
● **What kind of fruit is Jesus talking about?**
● **What does it mean to remain in Jesus?**
Have children take turns telling how they'll remain in Jesus this week.

"Remain in me, and I will remain in you. A branch cannot produce fruit alone but must remain in the vine. In the same way, you cannot produce fruit alone but must remain in me" (John 15:4).

MESSAGE BOARDS

"How beautiful is the person who comes over the mountains to bring good news, who announces peace and brings good news, who announces salvation and says to Jerusalem, 'Your God is King'" (Isaiah 52:7).

● ●

SUPPLIES

- ❑ twelve-inch lengths of one-by-six-inch pine
- ❑ four-inch strips of one-half-by-one-inch pine
- ❑ medium and fine-grain sandpaper
- ❑ sanding blocks or wood scraps
- ❑ tack cloth
- ❑ electric drill and quarter-inch bit
- ❑ wing nuts and screws
- ❑ newspaper
- ❑ spray paint or varnish
- ❑ bottled acrylic craft paints
- ❑ pencils with erasers
- ❑ matte acrylic sealer
- ❑ memo pads

This craft is a real crowd pleaser. Drills, bolts, and simple woodworking add up to a practical, fun-to-make message center. And the never-fail paint-dot flowers truly make every child an artist.

Plan to do this project outside to save on mess and avoid unpleasant fumes.

1. Have an adult drill two quarter-inch holes in the pine board and strips as shown in the illustration on page 19.

2. Give each child a twelve-inch length of board, a four-inch strip, and a piece of medium or fine-grain sandpaper attached to a sanding block or scrap of wood. Have kids sand all edges and surfaces, then wipe with a tack cloth.

3. Place the sanded wood on newspapers. Help kids finish the wood pieces with spray paint or spray varnish.

4. As the wood is drying, distribute bowls of acrylic craft paint and pencils with erasers. Let kids practice making paint-dot flowers on newspaper. Dip the eraser end of a pencil into the paint, then press a paint dot onto newspaper. That will be the center of the flower. Using another color of paint and a different pencil, make five dots around the center dot. When the wood pieces are dry, let kids decorate them with paint-dot flowers.

5. Allow the flowers to dry; then spray them lightly with matte acrylic sealer.

6. Have kids sandwich the top of a narrow memo pad between the twelve-inch board and the one-inch strip. Have them insert and tighten the wing nuts and screws to hold the memo pads in place.

FAITH BOOSTER

Have kids use the first page of their memo pads to write a message of good news from the Bible. Let kids copy Psalm 100:1-3 or another passage that tells of God's love and protection. Encourage kids to write favorite biblical verses on their memo boards from time to time to remind themselves and their families how much God loves us.

TOOTHPICK TOWERS

"Then they said to each other, 'Let's build a city and a tower for ourselves, whose top will reach high into the sky. We will become famous. Then we will not be scattered over all the earth'" (Genesis 11:4).

SUPPLIES

❑ miniature marshmallows
❑ round toothpicks
❑ cookie sheets

Tower building is fun for everyone. Do this craft as an individual or group project. Turn it into a game by seeing which group can build the highest tower in three minutes.

1. Form groups of four to six. Give each group a cookie sheet, a box of toothpicks, and a bag of miniature marshmallows.

2. Encourage each group to decide what kind of tower they'd like to build—a tall one, a skinny one, a fancy one, a round one, or a square one.

3. Give kids several minutes to work on their towers. Call time when all the marshmallows are used up!

4. Let kids display their towers and explain their special features.

FAITH BOOSTER

Ask:
● **What would you do if you wanted to show someone how great and talented and marvelous and awesome you are?**

Read Genesis 11:1-9. Ask:
● **Why did God stop the people from building their tower?**
● **When is it good to be proud of what we can do? When is it bad?**

Explain that God gives each person talents and abilities and that God is glad when we use those abilities to bring honor to him. Close by having kids use toothpicks and marshmallows to make letters that spell out, "God is great!"

PRO POINTER

Multicolored toothpicks and marshmallows make this project look even more impressive. For individual towers, use a paper plate rather than a cookie sheet to form the base.

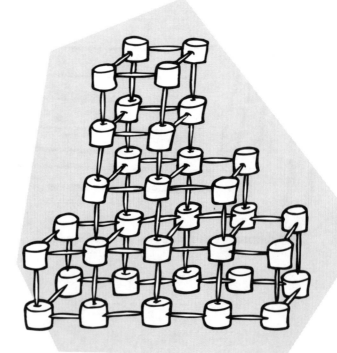

HEAVENLY HOMES

"There are many rooms in my Father's house; I would not tell you this if it were not true. I am going there to prepare a place for you" (John 14:2).

● ●

Constructing this craft will give kids a little taste of heaven!

1. Set out the "building materials" listed in the supply list. Form pairs, and give each pair a paper plate and a plastic knife.

2. Read the Scripture verse aloud; then challenge kids to use the materials you've set out to build models of what their homes in heaven might be like. Have an adult helper with a hot glue gun ready to assist with construction pieces that require a sturdier hold than the frosting and peanut butter provide.

3. Have kids place their completed projects on a table and admire each other's work.

FAITH BOOSTER

Have kids gather around their completed heavenly homes and close their eyes as you read the description of heaven from Revelation 21:10-25. Ask:

● **How is this description of heaven like your heavenly homes? How is it different?**

● **What do you think it will be like to live in heaven?**

● **Who is someone you're looking forward to seeing in heaven?**

● **How can we know that we're going to heaven?**

Close with a prayer of thanks for the hope of seeing Jesus in heaven someday.

SUPPLIES

❑ *sturdy paper plates*
❑ *sugar cubes*
❑ *marshmallows*
❑ *gum drops*
❑ *assorted hard candies*
❑ *canned frosting*
❑ *peanut butter*
❑ *plastic knives*
❑ *hot glue gun*

PRO POINTER

If you'd like these creations to remain edible, don't offer hot glue as a construction option.

MAP MODELING

"Pray for peace in Jerusalem: May those who love her be safe" (Psalm 122:6).

● ●

SUPPLIES

- ❑ topographical map of biblical lands
- ❑ heavy cardboard
- ❑ pencils
- ❑ mixing bowl
- ❑ flour
- ❑ salt
- ❑ water
- ❑ acrylic craft paints
- ❑ paintbrushes
- ❑ fine-point permanent markers
- ❑ matte acrylic sealer

Kids will love the fun and gooey experience of bringing biblical lands to life in a relief map that can remain in your class as an excellent teaching tool.

1. Have some kids take turns measuring and mixing dough in these proportions: one part flour, two parts salt, one part water. Add more water as needed until the dough is the consistency of cake frosting.

2. Help other kids refer to a topographical biblical map and sketch a map of biblical lands on a piece of heavy cardboard.

3. Let kids work together to build a relief map including mountains, rivers, and seas. High points on the map can be built up layer by layer.

4. After the map has dried for at least three days, let kids paint it with acrylic craft paints and use fine-point permanent markers to add names of countries, cities, rivers, and seas.

5. When the paint has dried, mist the map lightly with matte acrylic sealer. The map will keep indefinitely.

FAITH BOOSTER

Let kids mention several of their favorite biblical stories, then challenge them to locate on the map the places where the stories occurred. Bring in a modern world atlas, and compare the names and boundaries of ancient countries to current names and boundaries. Encourage kids to listen for the names of those countries in the news. Close by praying that God will bring peace to this troubled part of the world.

PAINT AND OTHER GOOD GOO

EXCELLENT SLIME

"He lifted me out of the slimy pit, out of the mud and mire; he set my feet on a rock and gave me a firm place to stand" (Psalm 40:2, NIV).

● ● ● ● ● ● ● ● ● ● ● ● ● ● ● ● ● ● ● ●

SUPPLIES

- ❑ wax paper
- ❑ safety pins
- ❑ measuring cups
- ❑ mixing bowls
- ❑ vegetable oil
- ❑ flour
- ❑ food coloring
- ❑ sandwich bags
- ❑ soap and water

Kneading and modeling with this slippery, slimy dough never fails to evoke delighted cries of "Gross!" and "Disgusting!" from kids.

1. Form groups of three or four. Hand out safety pins and twelve-inch lengths of wax paper. Explain that kids are about to have the privilege of creating something really gross, but first they'll need to pin on wax paper "bibs" to protect their clothing. Have kids help each other pin on their bibs and roll up their sleeves.

2. Give each group a measuring cup and a mixing bowl. Instruct kids to mix one-half cup of oil with three cups of flour and to take turns kneading their mixture. Allow them to add food coloring if they wish.

3. When the dough is smooth and easy to model, challenge kids to make slimy creations that remind them of difficult problems they've faced. For example, they might make a sad face, a house broken in two pieces, a nasty bug to represent being sick, or a storm cloud and raindrops.

4. When kids have finished, hand out sandwich bags for carrying home their creations.

FAITH BOOSTER

Have kids sit in a circle and place their creations in front of them. Read aloud Psalm 40:1-3 (NIV). Ask:

● **Who can tell about some of the slimy situations King David might have been thinking of when he wrote this psalm?**

● **What kinds of difficult, slimy situations do kids face today?**

● **Who can tell about a time God helped you get through a slimy situation?**

Close with a prayer thanking God that he doesn't leave us stuck in the mud, but helps us get through our problems and move on to better things.

PRO POINTER

Have kids use plenty of warm, soapy water for washing up.

WISER VISORS

"But you are a chosen people, royal priests, a holy nation, a people for God's own possession. You were chosen to tell about the wonderful acts of God, who called you out of darkness into his wonderful light" (1 Peter 2:9).

● ●

These sparkling creations are a snap to make and become the basis of a terrific affirmation activity.

1. Cover a table with newspapers. Set out visors, craft jewels, glitter paint, and washable markers.

2. Have children choose visors and write their first names on the brims with washable markers.

3. When kids are happy with the way their names look, have them trace over their names with glitter paint.

4. Demonstrate how to put a dot of glitter paint on a visor, then press a jewel into the paint. Let children choose a few jewels and attach them to their visors.

5. Set the visors in the sun to dry. Or speed the drying process with blow-dryers.

FAITH BOOSTER

Form a circle, and place a chair in the center. Read 1 Peter 2:9 aloud, and explain that when we ask Jesus to be our forever friend, we become royalty—sons and daughters of King Jesus! One by one, call children to sit on the chair. "Crown" each child with his or her visor as you say: **I crown you Prince (or Princess) (name of child).** Have the rest of the kids shout, "Long live Prince (or Princess) (name of child)!"

SUPPLIES

- ❑ *plastic visors in assorted colors*
- ❑ *washable markers*
- ❑ *tubes of glitter paint*
- ❑ *craft jewels*
- ❑ *newspaper*
- ❑ *optional: blow-dryers*

PRO POINTER

If kids are unhappy with the way their names look or if they smear the glitter paint, simply have them wash off the paint and begin again.

GOOPY SNOW DOUGH

"Jesus was born in the town of Bethlehem in Judea during the time when Herod was king" (Matthew 2:1).

SUPPLIES

- ❏ flour
- ❏ water
- ❏ measuring cups
- ❏ forks
- ❏ cotton balls
- ❏ optional: glitter
- ❏ small mixing bowls
- ❏ cookie sheets
- ❏ oven

Kids will enjoy making Christmas ornaments with this fun, lumpy modeling mixture.

1. Form groups of four to six. Give each group a mixing bowl, a fork, a measuring cup, a cookie sheet, and several cotton balls.

2. Have kids measure one cup of flour into their bowls and then carefully stir in about three-fourths to one cup of water. Explain that stirring in water a little at a time will help form a smooth paste.

3. Demonstrate how to dip cotton balls into the paste, place them together on a cookie sheet, and form them into Christmassy shapes such as stars, angels, snowflakes, or snowmen. Most shapes require three to six cotton balls.

4. If you wish, allow kids to decorate their shapes with glitter.

5. Bake the shapes at 325 degrees for one hour or until they're firm.

FAITH BOOSTER

Make a giant, sparkling "snowball" by patting an entire package of cotton balls into a round shape and wrapping the shape with a foil garland of stars or snowflakes. Have kids sit in a circle. Toss the snowball to a child, and ask a simple question about the story of Christmas, such as "Where was baby Jesus born?" or "Why did Mary and Joseph go to Bethlehem?" After the child answers, have him or her make up another question and toss the ball to another child. Be prepared to help kids think of questions.

PRO POINTER

Encourage kids to use a gentle touch as they form shapes so the cotton balls will stay light and puffy.

FOOTPRINT FUN

"When he brings all his sheep out, he goes ahead of them, and they follow him because they know his voice" (John 10:4).

● ● ● ● ● ● ● ● ● ● ● ● ● ● ● ●

Kids will have a foot-stompin' good time as they create a welcome banner which helps everyone step right up and join the fun. This is a great fall-kickoff craft!

1. Save on cleanup by doing this craft outside. Stretch and tape the fabric to a clean sidewalk. Set out pie pans filled one-half-inch deep with different colors of fabric paint.

2. Form pairs, and have kids remove their socks and shoes. Then explain that one person will be the Checker and one will be the Stomper.

3. Instruct the Stompers to place one foot carefully in a pan of fabric paint. Have them lift their feet so the Checkers can make sure the bottoms of their feet are evenly coated with paint.

4. Let the Checkers help the Stompers press their painted feet firmly on the fabric. Explain to kids that it's important to press hard and then lift their feet straight up without smudging the design.

5. Have each Stomper repeat the process with his or her other foot. Allow kids to use one or two colors of paint. When kids are finished painting, send them to the water hose to rinse the paint off their feet.

6. Let partners change roles to repeat the process.

7. Hand out fabric markers, and have kids sign the banner near their footprints. Encourage them to add Christian messages such as "Come follow Jesus" or "Join the Jesus Kids."

8. Keep a couple of pie pans and bottles of fabric paint on hand. When new kids join your group, make them feel welcome by inviting them to add their footprints and names to your banner.

FAITH BOOSTER

As the banner is drying, have kids scatter around your work area and sit on the ground. Read John 10:2-5 aloud. Then ask:
● **What do you think this story means?**
Explain that you're going to play a game which will help kids understand the story. Say that in a moment you'll ask everyone to close his or her eyes; then you'll tap a child on the shoulder and whisper a name. That child will say, "(Name of child), follow me." Then the child whose name was called can guess who the caller was.

Have kids close their eyes. Play the calling game until all the children have had their names called. Make the game more difficult for older kids by allowing callers to disguise their voices. Then ask:
● **Do you think Jesus knows your name? Why or why not?**
● **Why is it good to follow Jesus?**

SUPPLIES

- ❏ fabric marker
- ❏ fabric paint in bright colors
- ❏ pie pans
- ❏ two yards of light-colored fabric
- ❏ newspapers
- ❏ masking tape
- ❏ water hose
- ❏ old towels

PRO POINTER

This is also a great way to decorate vests, T-shirts, and sweat shirts. For best results, buy fabric and garments with high cotton content.

NAME-iN-A-RAiNBOW

"Now this is what the Lord says. He created you, people of Jacob; he formed you, people of Israel. He says, 'Don't be afraid, because I have saved you. I have called you by name, and you are mine'" (Isaiah 43:1).

● ●

SUPPLIES

- ❑ paper plates
- ❑ white crayons
- ❑ spray bottle and water
- ❑ containers of red, yellow, and blue tempera paints
- ❑ paintbrushes
- ❑ optional: blow-dryer

Kids are fascinated by the interplay of color as their names appear beneath a wash of rainbow hues.

1. Hand out paper plates and white crayons and have kids use white crayons to write their names (in fancy lettering, if they like) in the center of their plates.

2. Demonstrate how to lightly mist the plates with a spray of water. The plates should be damp, but there should be no puddles of water.

3. Set out containers of slightly thinned tempera paint. Show kids how to drop the three colors on their plates and swirl them just a bit with their paintbrushes.

4. As the paints dry, the white crayon will resist the paint, causing the names to appear beneath the rainbow colors. If you wish, speed the drying process with a blow-dryer.

FAITH BOOSTER

Distribute Bibles and have volunteers look up and read these verses that mention names with significant meanings: Genesis 17:5-6, 15-16; 20:3-6. Briefly review the story of Isaac's birth; then explain that the meaning of a name was very important in biblical times. Bring in a book of names and their meanings, and look up the names of the kids in your class. If a child's name is not given, have the other children help think of a meaning which reflects a positive attribute.

Read Isaiah 43:1, and explain that God knows our names and everything else about us. Mention that God loves us so much he sent Jesus to be our Savior. Present each child's plate to him or her as you say: (Name of child), **God has called you by name.**

PRO POINTER

Before craft time, experiment with thinning the tempera paint with enough water to allow the colors to mix and run together.

PAPER SLURP

"If anyone belongs to Christ, there is a new creation. The old things have gone; everything is made new!" (2 Corinthians 5:17).

● ● ● ● ● ● ● ● ● ● ● ● ● ● ● ● ●

Making recycled paper is great fun, and earth-friendly, too!

1. Tear paper into tiny bits and soak them in a bucket of water. You may want to put different types of paper (such as watercolor paper, newspaper, and construction paper) into different buckets. If possible, let the paper bits soak overnight to break down the fibers.

2. Have kids pour water and soaked paper bits into a blender. Run the blender until the paper is completely broken down into "slurp." WARNING: If the blender starts smelling hot, pour the liquid into another blender, and let the first one cool. *Always have adults supervise the operation of blenders.*

3. To drain excess liquid, place a paper coffee filter in a colander, and pour the paper slurp into the coffee filter.

4. When the excess water has drained, let kids scoop the paper slurp out of the coffee filter and pack it into seashells or other small molds.

5. Place the molds in an oven set on warm. Let them dry for two to three hours, or until the paper is dry to the touch.

6. Gently remove the paper forms from the molds.

FAITH BOOSTER

Ask:

● **If we hadn't used this paper to make something new, what would have happened to it?** Explain that you took what was used and useless and made something completely new. Say that the Bible tells us we can be made completely new again. Read 2 Corinthians 5:17 aloud. Then ask:

● **If you could change one thing about yourself, what would it be?**

Tell kids what you'd change if you could change one thing about yourself. Then ask volunteers to share their answers, but don't pressure anyone to share. Explain that a lot of people would like to be prettier, stronger, or smarter, but God changes us in more important ways. Ask:

● **What happens when God makes us new creatures?**

Close with prayer, thanking God for making us new and clean on the inside.

SUPPLIES

- ❑ used paper
- ❑ buckets
- ❑ water
- ❑ electric blenders
- ❑ seashells
- ❑ small molds
- ❑ colander
- ❑ paper coffee filters
- ❑ oven
- ❑ optional: watercolor paper, newspaper, and construction paper

PRO POINTER

The finished paper forms may be mounted on heavy paper or mat board for display, or used to embellish frames, packages, or boxes.

PLASTER CASTERS

"Make your father and mother happy; give your mother a reason to be glad" (Proverbs 23:25).

● ●

SUPPLIES

- ❑ plaster of Paris
- ❑ mixing bowl
- ❑ plastic spoons
- ❑ plastic knives
- ❑ pin backs
- ❑ acrylic craft paints
- ❑ paintbrushes
- ❑ spray gloss varnish
- ❑ optional: glue, pressed flowers

This classic craft can be fancy or funky; either way, it makes a great Mother's Day gift.

1. Mix the plaster of Paris according to package instructions.
2. Have each child fill a plastic spoon with plaster and smooth the top with a knife so the plaster is level with the edge of the spoon.
3. Help each child press a pin back into the plaster. Let the plaster harden for at least an hour.
4. Demonstrate how to pop the plaster shapes out of the spoons.
5. Set out paints and brushes. Let kids paint their choice of designs, such as hearts, flowers, polka dots, or bugs.
6. When the brooches are dry, take them outside and spray them with varnish.

FAITH BOOSTER

Read Proverbs 23:25 aloud. Ask:
- **What things about you make your mother glad?**
- **What things about your mother make you glad?**

Let kids cut or tear hearts from construction paper. Have them write, "Mom, thank you for…," and list things they appreciate. Encourage kids to write both serious and funny comments. Have them pin the brooches to the hearts.

PRO POINTER

If you have access to pressed flowers, you may want to have kids brush a thin layer of glue on the brooches, then press flowers carefully into the glue.

FABULOUS FACE PAINT

"Lord, you have made many things; with your wisdom you made them all. The earth is full of your riches" (Psalm 104:24).

● ● ● ● ● ● ● ● ● ● ● ● ● ● ● ● ●

Face painting brings out the animal in your kids!

1. Let kids decide what animal they'd like to be. Easily painted animal faces include zebras, leopards, cows, cats, and fish.

2. Have older kids or extra adult helpers serve as makeup artists. Use any combination of cosmetics and brushes or cotton swabs to create animal faces.

3. Set out construction paper, cotton balls, scissors, and tape. Let kids use acrylic craft paint to create ears, noses, and manes to accessorize their beastly looks.

4. Be sure to "capture" your wild beasts on film before kids use cleansing cream to remove the cosmetics.

FAITH BOOSTER

Read aloud Psalm 104:10-30. Have children take turns telling what their animals eat, what kind of homes they live in, and how God provides for them. Ask:

● **Why does God bother watching over wild animals?**

● **What can we do to help care for animals?**

● **If God watches over animals, what will he do for us?**

Give your animals a snack of "hay"—frosted shredded wheat biscuits, and let them try lapping juice from paper cups.

SUPPLIES

❑ acrylic craft paint
❑ assorted cosmetics
❑ soft paintbrushes
❑ cotton swabs
❑ cotton balls
❑ construction paper
❑ scissors
❑ tape
❑ cleansing cream
❑ optional: camera

PRO POINTER

It's a good idea to have kids keep their eyes closed as you apply makeup.

MARBELOUS MARBLING

"'I know what I am planning for you,' says the Lord. 'I have good plans for you, not plans to hurt you. I will give you hope and a good future'" (Jeremiah 29:11b).

● ●

SUPPLIES

☐ *liquid starch*
☐ *glass cake pans*
☐ *acrylic craft paint*
☐ *hair picks*
☐ *heavy paper*
☐ *water*

The ancient art of marbling becomes quite accessible to kids with this simplified technique. Since no two papers come out alike, the process is fun and exciting!

1. Pour liquid starch into glass cake pans to a depth of one and one-half inches. Prepare one pan for every five to six kids.

2. Let children squeeze little pools of three colors of acrylic paint onto the surface of the starch.

3. Demonstrate how to use a hair pick to carefully "comb" the colors into an interesting pattern. Be sure kids don't push the paint down into the starch—it must remain on the surface.

4. Have kids take turns carefully laying a sheet of heavy paper on the surface of the starch. Encourage kids to press the paper *gently* so no air bubbles remain between the paper and the surface.

5. Show kids how to lift the paper and rinse off the starch under a stream of water. A beautiful marbled design will remain on the paper.

6. Before the next child has a turn, have him or her drag a sheet of scrap paper across the surface of the starch to pick up any remaining paint. Then have kids add new puddles of color and start again.

PRO POINTER

You can make beautiful marbled cards with a box of plain note cards and envelopes. Press only the top and bottom edges of the note cards into the paint to make marbled borders. Press only the flap of the envelopes into the paint. Voilà!

FAITH BOOSTER

As the marbled papers are drying, gather kids and ask:
● **What was it like to see a beautiful design appear on your papers?**
● **Could you plan exactly how they would turn out? Why or why not?**

Say that one reason it's fun to do marbling is because each new paper is a surprise and no two papers are exactly alike. Explain how our lives are similar—no two days are exactly alike. Happy days are like the bright colors in the marbling pan. Unhappy days are like darker colors that run into the bright ones and try to cover them up. Even though we don't know what each new day will bring, we can put our faith in someone who does. Read Jeremiah 29:11 aloud, then ask:
● **What kinds of plans does God have for us?**
● **What good things has God planned for your life so far?**
● **How can we trust God's plans for the future?**

MONOGRAM MANIA

"God made us his chosen people. He put his mark on us to show that we are his, and he put his Spirit in our hearts to be a guarantee for all he has promised" (2 Corinthians 1:21b-22).

● ●

SUPPLIES

- ❑ tracing paper
- ❑ graphite transfer paper
- ❑ pencils
- ❑ tape
- ❑ glitter glue
- ❑ slick paint
- ❑ metallic markers
- ❑ items of your choice to be monogrammed

PRO POINTER

A traditional monogram consists of a large letter for the initial of the last name, and small letters on both sides of the larger one for the first and middle name initials.

We all identify closely with our names, so a personalized gift—to ourselves or a loved one— always feels special.

1. Photocopy the monogram patterns (p. 35). Cut tracing paper into three-inch squares. Let kids use pencils to trace the letters they want to use in their monograms.

2. Have kids position the traced-letter squares and secure the tracing paper with a piece of tape.

3. Demonstrate how to slip a piece of transfer paper under the tracing paper, then let kids trace over their letters once again.

4. Have kids remove the tracing paper and transfer paper, and then use glitter glue, slick paint, or metallic markers to write over the transferred letters.

FAITH BOOSTER

Ask:
- ● **What's special about having your initials on something?**
- ● **What things at home have your name or initials on them? at school?**

Explain that the Bible tells about a special mark God puts on us to show that we are his people. Read 2 Corinthians 1:21b-22 aloud. Ask:
- ● **What kind of "mark" do you think this verse is talking about?**
- ● **How can you tell if another person is a Christian?**
- ● **How can someone tell that you belong to God?**

ABCDEFGHIJ
KLMNOPQRS
TUVWXYZ

ABCDEFGHIJ
KLMNOPQRS
TUVWXYZ

SPATTER MATTERS

"Let the fields and everything in them rejoice. Then all the trees of the forest will sing for joy before the Lord, because he is coming" (Psalm 96:12-13a).

SUPPLIES

- ❑ *ivory card stock*
- ❑ *scissors*
- ❑ *red and green tempera paint*
- ❑ *leaves and sprigs of pine*
- ❑ *toothbrushes*
- ❑ *newspaper*

Spatter painting items from nature creates exquisite Christmas cards and is simple enough for even the youngest crafters!

1. Lead kids on a short walk to find leaves and sprigs of pine.
2. Help kids cut and fold the ivory card stock into cards.
3. Cover your work area with newspaper. Set out tempera paint and toothbrushes.
4. Demonstrate how to place a leaf or sprig on a card, dip a toothbrush into paint, and then slide your thumb or finger over the bristles of the toothbrush so the paint sprays and splatters on the card. Repeat the process until the leaf or sprig is completely surrounded by paint.
5. Carefully lift the leaf and its outline will be revealed.

FAITH BOOSTER

Read aloud Psalm 96:10-13. Ask:
- **Why does this psalm tell us to rejoice?**
- **Who does it say is coming to judge the world?**
- **Who came to the world at Christmas?**

Explain that using designs from leaves and twigs to spread Christmas cheer is one way to let the trees of the forest "sing for joy." Encourage kids to write joyful Christmas messages in their cards.

PRO POINTER

With older children, you may want to use metallic acrylic paint slightly thinned with water.

GOOD NEWS GRAFFITI

"We cannot keep quiet. We must speak about what we have seen and heard" (Acts 4:20).

● ●

Painting a wall of their room gives kids a special sense of ownership and allows a creative outlet for sharing their faith.

1. Obtain permission to decorate a wall of your meeting area. Begin this activity with the Faith Booster outlined below.

2. Have kids brainstorm and work together to create a large design which will allow space for individuals to add their own personal touch. For example, kids might choose to paint a large cross or a message such as "Jesus Is Good News."

3. Help kids sketch their design on the wall with pencils. Protect the area beneath your painting with masking tape and dropcloths.

4. When the design is finished, allow kids to paint their own names and personal additions—be sure kids clear their ideas with you before they paint.

FAITH BOOSTER

Appoint two kids to be Peter and John, another to be the captain, and another to be the high priest. Have the rest of the kids be Sadducees and the soldiers. Read aloud Acts 4:1-20, cueing kids to act out their parts as they listen. Then ask:

● **What punishment would Peter and John receive if they kept on telling about Jesus?**

● **How did Peter and John respond to the order not to tell anyone else about Jesus?**

● **Why weren't they afraid?**

● **How can we continue to tell the good news about Jesus?**

Explain that the class is about to embark on a special painting project that will encourage kids to keep telling the good news.

SUPPLIES

❑ *leftover paint in several colors*

❑ *paintbrushes*

❑ *pencils*

❑ *masking tape*

❑ *dropcloths*

PRO POINTER

You may wish to invite parents to a special punch-and-cookies reception and viewing of the wall.

ROCK CRITTERS

"Tell them the water stopped flowing in the Jordan when the Ark of the Agreement with the Lord crossed the river. These rocks will always remind the Israelites of this" (Joshua 4:7).

● ●

SUPPLIES

- ☐ small rocks
- ☐ coloring books with pictures of animals
- ☐ scissors
- ☐ white paper
- ☐ lids from whipped topping tubs
- ☐ water
- ☐ water containers
- ☐ pencils
- ☐ acrylic craft paints
- ☐ paintbrushes
- ☐ spray bottles
- ☐ acrylic matte sealer

A little imagination and acrylic paint transforms plain rocks into cute critters.

1. Lead kids on a rock hunt, and let them choose one or two small, smooth rocks. Rinse the rocks at an outdoor faucet.

2. Before craft time or as children are hunting, prepare moist palettes by cutting clean white paper so it fits inside the plastic lids. Place the paper in the lids and add about one-third inch of water. Allow the paper to soak up as much water as possible.

3. Set out coloring books of animals as inspiration. Let children use pencils to sketch on their rocks the animals they "see."

4. As children are sketching, pour the excess water off the palettes, then squeeze several paint puddles of acrylic paint onto each palette.

5. Let children paint colorful critters on their rocks. Some colors may require two or three coats of paint for coverage.

6. After the rocks have dried, mist them with acrylic matte sealer.

FAITH BOOSTER

Ask:
● **What are some different ways we use rocks?**
Tell kids how Joshua used rocks in a very special way when God's people crossed the Jordan river. Tell the story from Joshua 4, and read 4:7. Ask:
● **What was special about the twelve rocks God's people put in their camp?**
● **Who can tell about a time God did something very special for you?**
Encourage kids to use their rock critters to remind them of special things God does in their lives.

PRO POINTER

Acrylic paint dries very rapidly, even on a moist palette. To keep the paint workable, mist the palettes with a spray bottle every two or three minutes.

MARVELOUS MUNCHABLES

DOUGH-LIGHTFUL DISCOVERIES

"You made my whole being; you formed me in my mother's body. I praise you because you made me in an amazing and wonderful way" (Psalm 139:13-14a).

● ●

SUPPLIES

- ❑ peanut butter
- ❑ small mixing bowls
- ❑ powdered sugar
- ❑ plastic knives
- ❑ wax paper
- ❑ optional: butter and vanilla flavoring

PRO POINTER

If you're a peanut butter connoisseur, add just a bit of butter and vanilla flavoring to the dough. Mmm-mmm! (Warning: this dough melts in your mouth like the inside of a peanut butter cup and can be addictive!)

This peanut butter dough craft is irresistibly delicious and becomes the basis for a wonderful community-building activity.

1. Since measuring peanut butter is messy, plan to do it ahead of time. Place three-fourths cup of peanut butter in small mixing bowls. You'll need one bowl for every four kids.

2. Form groups of four. Let kids measure and add three-fourths cup of powdered sugar to their bowls.

3. Demonstrate how to mix the peanut butter and powdered sugar by cutting through the peanut butter with a plastic knife and turning it over, as if you were mixing pastry dough. Let kids take turns mixing until their dough is smooth and not too sticky. You may need to help them add a bit more powdered sugar to achieve the right consistency.

4. When the dough is smooth, let kids divide it among themselves. Give each child a small square of wax paper to work on. Ask children to model their dough into something that tells about who they are. For instance, they might model a pair of ballet slippers, a baseball and bat, a musical instrument, or a stack of books.

FAITH BOOSTER

Have kids sit in circles with their groups. Encourage them to tell their group members about what they made and why it's important to them. After groups have shared, call everyone together. Invite kids to tell what they learned about each other.

Read Psalm 139:13-16 aloud. Explain that God made each of us special and even though we have different interests and abilities, God loves each one of us.

Close with a dough-gobbling feast!

PITA PORTRAITS

"But you are a shield around me, O Lord; you bestow glory on me and lift up my head" (Psalm 3:3, NIV).

● ●

Picture this—a gallery of portraits made on pita bread with yummy ingredients of your choice. Kids will love it!

1. Give each child pita bread on a paper plate. Set out the rest of the ingredients.
2. Invite kids to use any or all of the ingredients to make self-portraits. Encourage them to make portraits that really look like themselves and not to let others see their work.
3. Have kids bring their finished portraits to you. Set them out in a random display.
4. When everyone has finished, gather kids and display the portraits one by one. Let kids guess whose portrait you're holding.
5. Let kids decide whether to eat their portraits or take them home to show their families.

FAITH BOOSTER

Have a silly face contest. Call out emotions, such as surprise, anger, excitement, and sadness. After you call out each emotion, point to three or four children who are making the most interesting faces, and have them stand. Ask the children who are standing:

● **What makes you feel the way you look right now?**

Allow other children to tell about times they felt that way. Ask all the kids to change their sad faces to happy ones as you read Psalm 3:3 aloud. Ask:

● **How does God help us get happy when we're sad and discouraged?**

Invite kids to tell how God has helped them in sad times. Encourage kids to remember this verse when they're feeling down.

SUPPLIES

❑ paper plates
❑ pita bread
❑ peanut butter
❑ plastic knives
your choice of:
❑ raisins
❑ olives
❑ fruit leather
❑ jelly
❑ shredded cheese
❑ string licorice
❑ apple rings
❑ banana slices
❑ carrot curls

PRO POINTER

Choose only the ingredients that are easy and convenient for you to bring. You may wish to slit pita bread around the edge and give kids half a pita to work on.

JEWEL COOKIE CROWNS

"Gray hair is like a crown of honor; it is earned by living a good life" (Proverbs 16:31).

● ●

SUPPLIES

- ❑ sugar-cookie dough
- ❑ plastic knives
- ❑ canned frosting
- ❑ small gumdrops
- ❑ decorative sprinkles
- ❑ nonpareils
- ❑ cookie sheets
- ❑ resealable sandwich bags
- ❑ wax paper
- ❑ oven

PRO POINTER

You may want to simplify this craft by using pre-baked cookies. Or let kids take over the kitchen as they learn to be "cookie chefs" and make dough and frosting from scratch.

No treat is quite as good as a shared treat! Use this bejeweled cookie craft to help kids understand that their kindness can make a difference in the lives of others.

1. Before craft time, make arrangements to visit the homes of elderly people in your congregation or a class of senior citizens that meets in your church.

2. Preheat an oven as kids slice or press cookie dough into rounds. Place cookies on cookie sheets, and bake according to package directions.

3. While the cookies bake, do the Faith Booster described below.

4. When the cookies have cooled, have each child take a sheet of wax paper and at least two cookies to decorate (so they'll have one to share and one to eat). Let kids use the frosting, gumdrops, sprinkles, and nonpareils to turn their cookies into sparkling crowns.

5. Slip the finished crowns into resealable sandwich bags, and have kids deliver them.

FAITH BOOSTER

Ask:
- ● **What do you think it feels like to get older?**
- ● **What kinds of things are difficult for older people to do?**

Read Proverbs 16:31 aloud. Ask:
- ● **Do you think the older people you know feel honored?**

Talk about what it feels like to grow older and gradually lose physical abilities. Encourage kids to tell about their elderly relatives or neighbors. Explain that older folks often feel pushed aside and appreciate it when people take time to pay attention to them. Tell kids about your plans to share the cookie crowns they're making. Encourage kids to be warm and friendly as they deliver their treats.

RED SEA FONDUE

"Then Moses and the Israelites sang this song to the Lord: 'I will sing to the Lord, because he is worthy of great honor. He has thrown the horse and its rider into the sea'" (Exodus 15:1).

● ●

If you're looking for an excuse for a chocolate feast, here it is! Use this story enhancer to act out what happened to the Israelites and Pharaoh's army as they crossed the Red Sea.

1. Have kids help you place one stick of butter, twelve ounces of chocolate chips, one can of sweetened condensed milk, and several drops of food coloring in a glass cake pan.

2. Cover the pan with wax paper and place it in a microwave oven. Cook it at 50 percent power, stopping the oven every thirty seconds to let kids take turns stirring the mixture.

3. When the mixture is completely blended and bubbly, take it out of the oven and let it cool for a minute or two.

FAITH BOOSTER

Let kids take turns spearing dippers with toothpicks, dragging them through the "Red Sea," and gobbling them up. Explain that the dippers are like the Israelites who crossed the Red Sea safely. After all the kids have had two or three dippers, heat the chocolate mixture for a few seconds, then toss in a cup of crisp rice cereal and have the children help you stir it in with a wooden spoon. Explain that the Egyptian soldiers who tried to go after the Israelites got swallowed up by the sea, just like the rice cereal was swallowed up in the fondue. Serve each child a dollop of the chocolate-rice cereal combination on a square of wax paper. Close by reading Exodus 15:1 and singing a song such as "Horse and Rider."

SUPPLIES

❑ butter
❑ chocolate chips
❑ sweetened condensed milk
❑ red food coloring
❑ glass cake pan
❑ wax paper
❑ toothpicks
❑ crisp rice cereal
❑ wooden spoon
your choice of "dippers":
❑ marshmallows
❑ mandarin orange sections
❑ strawberries
❑ banana chunks

PRO POINTER

If kids touch the toothpicks with their mouths, give them fresh toothpicks for each round of dipping.

STAINED GLASS CANDY MOSAICS

"Lord All-Powerful, how lovely is your Temple! I want more than anything to be in the court-yards of the Lord's Temple. My whole being wants to be with the living God" (Psalm 84:1-2).

● ●

SUPPLIES

- ❏ glass cake or pie pans
- ❏ bowls
- ❏ corn syrup
- ❏ small paper cups
- ❏ toothpicks

your choice of hard candies:

- ❏ Life Savers
- ❏ M&M's
- ❏ Good & Plenty
- ❏ butterscotch drops
- ❏ peppermints

In this unique craft, kids transform sweet treats into glowing works of art.

1. Form groups of four to six. Give each group a glass cake or pie pan, a bowl of assorted candies, a small cup of corn syrup, and several toothpicks.

2. Let each group choose a word or symbol from the Bible to illustrate using the candies to form a mosaic design. For example, kids might form a dove, a cross, or create the word "joy."

3. Demonstrate how to pick up a drop of corn syrup with a toothpick, touch it to the back of a hard candy, and press it into place in a design.

4. When kids have finished, have them hold their creations in front of a bright window or light bulb as they explain the significance of their designs.

FAITH BOOSTER

Read aloud Psalm 84:1-10. Explain that in biblical times, faithful Jews traveled to Jerusalem three times a year to celebrate and to worship at the Temple. Everyone looked forward to these holidays and they sang songs, such as Psalm 84, as they traveled. Ask:

- ● **When do you really look forward to coming to our church?**
- ● **What's your favorite church celebration?**

Show illustrations of Jerusalem and the Temple. Talk about how places of worship have changed over the centuries. Display pictures of gothic cathedrals and point out how the beautiful stained glass is similar to the glowing mosaics the kids just finished. Close by reading Psalm 84:10. Encourage kids to be joyful every time they come to worship God.

PRO POINTER

Warn kids not to hold their designs so they're completely vertical, but to keep them tipped back in case the corn syrup "glue" hasn't quite dried.

GARDEN OF EDEN DIRT SOUFFLÉ

"Then the Lord God planted a garden in the east, in a place called Eden" (Genesis 2:8a).

● ●

More fun than mud pies! Kids will delight in customizing their own mini-gardens.

1. Form groups of four to six. Give each group a quart jar with a lid, pudding mix, two cups of milk, chocolate sandwich cookies in a strong resealable plastic bag, a rolling pin, plastic spoons, and a clay pot. Set the animal crackers, gummy worms, and jelly beans on a table where all the groups will have access to them.

2. Have each group choose people to be Pudding Shakers and Cookie Crushers. Instruct the Pudding Shakers to pour the milk and pudding mix into the quart jar, tightly screw on the lid, and shake the jars for three minutes.

3. Meanwhile, have the Cookie Crushers roll the rolling pins over the sealed bags to make cookie-crumb "dirt."

4. When the pudding is made and the cookies are crushed, gather kids and do the Faith Booster below.

5. Invite each group to create a "Garden of Eden" in their clay pot. Let them layer the pudding and cookie dirt, help themselves to crackers and worms, and use the jelly beans as flowers.

6. When the gardens are complete, let kids admire each other's work. Then let each child "dig in" to the gardens, scoop a generous helping into a paper cup, and gobble!

FAITH BOOSTER

Ask:
● **What do you know about the Garden of Eden?**
Read aloud Genesis 2:4-9. Ask:
● **What do you think it would have been like to live in that garden?**
● **What's the most beautiful garden you've ever seen?**
Let volunteers tell why Adam and Eve had to leave the garden. Explain that many people have looked for the Garden of Eden, but no one knows exactly where it was. Tell kids we can imagine what the Garden of Eden was like and we'll have some creative fun making Garden of Eden Dirt Soufflés.

SUPPLIES

❑ *quart jars with lids*
❑ *instant chocolate pudding mix*
❑ *milk*
❑ *chocolate sandwich cookies*
❑ *strong resealable plastic bags*
❑ *rolling pins*
❑ *plastic spoons*
❑ *new, small clay pots*
❑ *animal crackers*
❑ *gummy worms*
❑ *small jelly beans*
❑ *paper cups*

PRO POINTER

You may want to let kids spoon the leftovers into resealable bags and take the bags home.

WALLS OF JERICHO

"When the priests blew the trumpets, the people shouted. At the sound of the trumpets and the people's shout, the walls fell" (Joshua 6:20a).

SUPPLIES

- ❏ graham crackers
- ❏ marshmallow creme
- ❏ marshmallows
- ❏ gumdrops
- ❏ plastic knives
- ❏ M&M's
- ❏ sandwich bags

PRO POINTER

You may wish to invite parents to view the completed wall and to help bring it down!

Just like the real thing, these walls are built to tumble down!

1. Begin by doing the Faith Booster below.
2. Gather kids around a clean table where you've set out graham crackers, marshmallow creme, marshmallows and gumdrops. Depending on the size of your table and the number of kids in your group, decide how many graham crackers each person can add to the wall.
3. Have kids brainstorm about different ways to build the wall and vote on the group's preferred method.
4. Using marshmallow creme as mortar, have kids build the wall and embellish it with marshmallows and candies.
5. Lead kids in marching around the wall seven times, and shouting, "For the Lord and for Joshua!" Let kids stomp on the floor and shake the table until the wall comes down. Cheer and clap; then let kids take their own parts of the wall home in sandwich bags.

FAITH BOOSTER

Explain that in Old Testament times, important cities were surrounded by walls that kept out invaders. Jericho was one of the oldest walled cities in the world and was the first city in the Promised Land that Joshua and the Israelites had to conquer. Read aloud Joshua 6:1-5. Ask:

- **What do you think about God's plan for conquering the city?**
- **Why do you think God gave Joshua this strange plan?**

Read aloud Joshua 6:6-20. Explain that you're going to build the walls of Jericho and see if you can bring them down just as Joshua did.

SNOWFLAKE CRUSTS

"Take away my sin, and I will be clean. Wash me, and I will be whiter than snow" (Psalm 51:7).

● ●

As they make these delicious treats, children will learn an important lesson about forgiveness.

1. Give each child a small lump of pie crust dough on wax paper.

2. Show kids how to dust their hands lightly with flour and then pat the dough into a flat circle.

3. Have kids dust the circle with flour, fold it in half, and cut out shapes to form a snowflake design.

4. Demonstrate how to open the circle and then fold it in half the other way and cut out more shapes.

5. Have kids sprinkle their snowflakes with sugar and transfer them to cookie sheets.

6. Bake the snowflakes at 425 degrees until they're lightly browned. Cool and eat!

FAITH BOOSTER

As the snowflakes are cooling, gather kids in a circle. Rub a piece of charcoal between your hands, and tell kids you're thinking of a time when you sinned and did something that displeased God. Then toss the charcoal to a child and ask him or her to think of a time he or she sinned. Continue until each person has rubbed their hands with the charcoal and silently thought about a sin. Ask:

● **How do your hands feel?**

● **How is that like how you feel inside when you've sinned?**

Tell kids you're going to read what King David wrote after he had stolen another man's wife. Read aloud Psalm 51:1-9. Then lead kids to a sink, and let them wash their hands with soap and water. Dry each child's hands, and say: (Name of child), **God can make your heart as white as snow.**

Before you eat the pie-crust snowflakes, thank God for his wonderful gift of forgiveness.

SUPPLIES

❑ refrigerated pie crust dough

❑ wax paper

❑ flour

❑ plastic knives

❑ sugar

❑ cookie sheets

PRO POINTER

You may want to teach kids to make their own dough for pie crust. Here's a great recipe: In a bowl, mix 2⅓ cups flour, 1 teaspoon salt, ½ cup plus 1 tablespoon oil, and ¼ cup plus 1 tablespoon milk.

ROBINS' NESTS

"Good news makes you feel better. Your happiness will show in your eyes" (Proverbs 15:30).

● ●

SUPPLIES

- ❑ margarine
- ❑ marshmallow creme
- ❑ peanut butter
- ❑ chow mein noodles
- ❑ mixing bowl
- ❑ wax paper
- ❑ jelly beans or malted candy bird's eggs

These unique springtime treats are as beautiful as they are delicious. Use them as favors for an Easter brunch.

1. Form groups of six. Give each group two tablespoons of melted margarine, one seven-ounce jar of marshmallow creme, one-fourth cup of peanut butter, three cups of chow mein noodles, and a mixing bowl.

2. Have groups stir the peanut butter and margarine together, then add the marshmallow creme and chow mein noodles.

3. Show kids how to grease their fingers with margarine, then form the mixture into nests and set them on wax paper. There should be enough for each child to make two or three nests.

4. After kids have washed their hands, let them drop two or three jelly beans or candy eggs into each nest.

FAITH BOOSTER

Read Proverbs 15:30 aloud. Ask:

- ● **Who can tell about a time you got good news?**
- ● **Who can tell about a time you got a good surprise?**

Explain that springtime is good news because blossoming trees and flowers, new grass, and baby animals remind us that Jesus rose from the dead. Go "spring caroling" to another class. Sing these words to the tune of "Row, Row, Row Your Boat" and be sure to take your treats to share!

Spring, spring, spring has come,
Winter's gone at last.
You'd better come and eat our treats
Because they're going fast!

PRO POINTER

If you have a microwave oven nearby, you may want to have kids heat the peanut butter and margarine mixture for a few seconds so they'll blend easily.

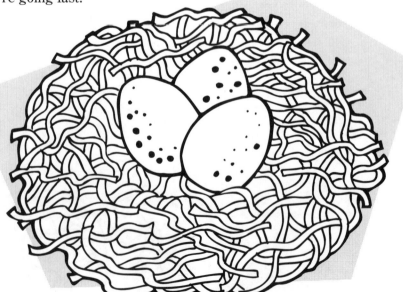

PUDDING STORIES

"How sweet are your words to my taste, sweeter than honey to my mouth" (Psalm 119:103, NIV).

● ●

Whenever I've let preschoolers dive into a pudding painting, older kids cry, "No fair—we want to do that." So let them! And use this "goo-licious" craft to introduce your kids to the joy of serving.

1. Before craft time, arrange to have a class of preschoolers visit your group.

2. Form groups of six. Have some kids mix pudding and milk in quart jars while others distribute a plastic spoon and an eighteen-inch length of wax paper to each person.

3. Let each group choose a Bible story to illustrate with "pudding paint" and plan their illustrations so that each length of wax paper becomes a new page of the story.

4. Using plastic spoons as drawing instruments, have kids create their story illustrations with pudding.

FAITH BOOSTER

When the pudding artists have finished, gather them in a circle, and read Psalm 119:103 aloud. Explain that God's words are so sweet that we want to share them with others. Have kids go with you to bring groups of preschoolers to your room. Let your kids tell their Bible stories as the little ones observe the pudding paintings. Then mark off portions of the paintings for each person to eat!

SUPPLIES

❑ chocolate, vanilla, and pistachio instant pudding mixes
❑ quart jars with lids
❑ milk
❑ plastic spoons
❑ wax paper

PRO POINTER

You may want to add other colors to your "pudding palette" by mixing food coloring with vanilla pudding.

LICORICE LUMP ZOO

"Noah did everything that God commanded him" (Genesis 6:22).

● ● ● ● ● ● ● ● ● ● ● ● ● ● ● ● ● ● ●

SUPPLIES

❑ soft, rope licorice (Pull-n-Peel Twizzlers work well)

❑ graham crackers

❑ peanut butter

❑ plastic knives

❑ small marshmallows

❑ small pretzel sticks

It was kids in vacation Bible school who taught me about the wonderful sculpting possibilities of soft rope licorice (when they were supposed to be doing something else, of course).

1. Gather everyone in a circle. Have kids take turns telling you the story of Noah and the ark, a few words at a time. "Pay" kids a rope of licorice when they've added to the story, but be sure they don't eat the licorice yet.

2. When you've given licorice to everyone, have kids press their licorice into balls. Let kids raise their hands, call out which pair of animals they'd like to make, and sculpt those animals.

3. Set out graham crackers, marshmallows, and small pretzel sticks. Make a sample "cage" by spreading peanut butter around the edge of a graham cracker, sticking marshmallows into the peanut butter, and pushing pretzel stick "bars" into the marshmallows.

4. When kids have finished their animals, have them make cages and set the animals inside.

5. Let kids assemble all the cages into the shape of an ark.

PRO POINTER

If you can't find soft licorice, substitute the peanut butter dough recipe from the "Dough-lightful Discoveries" activity (p. 40).

FAITH BOOSTER

Read Genesis 6:22 aloud. Ask:

● **How do you think Noah felt when God asked him to build a huge boat far away from any lake or sea?**

● **What kinds of hard things does God ask us to do today?**

Mention things such as being nice to someone who's always mean at school; believing that God hears our prayers; making friends with someone who's always left out; and obeying parents even when we think they're being unfair.

Read Genesis 7:8 aloud. Point out that Noah didn't have to go hunting—God brought the animals to him. Explain that when God asks us to do something hard, he always helps us, just as he helped Noah.

GUMDROP COOKIE BOUQUETS

"The desert will be glad and will produce flowers. Like a flower, it will have many blooms. It will show its happiness, as if it were shouting with joy" (Isaiah 35:1b-2a).

● ●

What better way to spread joy than with bouquets that are both beautiful and delicious!

1. Form groups of six. Give each group a large ball of sugar-cookie dough and a cookie sheet. Have kids pat the dough into a circle on the cookie sheet. Bake the cookies according to the recipe.

2. As the cookies bake, demonstrate how to place gumdrops between sheets of wax paper and roll them flat with a rolling pin. Peel away the wax paper and cut the flattened gumdrops into flower petals, or cut them into strips and roll them up like rosebuds. Use green gumdrops to make leaves and stems.

3. Give each group a rolling pin or smooth-edged jar, wax paper, and several gumdrops. Invite kids to invent their own gumdrop flowers.

4. When the cookies have cooled, place them on paper plates and let kids spread frosting on them, then "plant" their gardens of gumdrop flowers.

FAITH BOOSTER

Gather kids in a circle and read Isaiah 35:1-2 aloud. Explain that the prophet Isaiah wrote these words to comfort God's people who had been carried off to their enemies' homeland while their own land of Israel lay in ruins. The prophet wanted God's people to know that their hard times would end, and that God would bless them again. Ask:

● **Who do you know who's going through hard times right now?**

● **Who do you think might be encouraged to receive one of our cookie bouquets?**

Let kids decide who should receive their treats. If you wish, have the kids who made each bouquet write an encouraging note and sign it. Place the finished bouquets on paper plates and help kids deliver them.

SUPPLIES

- ❏ sugar-cookie dough
- ❏ cookie sheets
- ❏ gumdrops
- ❏ wax paper
- ❏ rolling pin
- ❏ plastic knives
- ❏ canned frosting
- ❏ paper plates

PRO POINTER

You may want to allow kids to use clean scissors to cut the flattened gumdrops.

FABULOUS FIBERS

FEATHER AND LEATHER CROSSES

"But he was wounded for the wrong we did; he was crushed for the evil we did. The punishment, which made us well, was given to him, and we are healed because of his wounds" (Isaiah 53:5).

● ●

These unique crosses from natural materials provide thought-provoking reminders of Jesus' sacrifice.

    1. Form pairs. Pair kids who know how to make square knots with those who don't. (You may need to demonstrate how to make square knots.) Give each child a twenty-two-inch length of leather shoelace and a generous yard of jute twine.

    2. Have one partner fold a leather lace in the middle. Show the other partner how to wrap the twine around the lace one inch from the fold and tie three square knots with the twine. This creates a loop at the top of the lace.

    3. With the first partner holding the loop, have the second partner place two four-inch twigs snugly beneath the last square knot to form the crossbar. The lace should be on top of the twigs and the twine should be behind them.

    4. Below the twigs, have kids tie seven more square knots with the twine. Then instruct partners to trade roles and work on the second cross.

    5. Slide the quill of a bird feather or craft feather into the last knot so the feather is pointing down. Reinforce the last knot with glue. Trim the ends of the lace and twine to the desired length, and ravel the twine.

FAITH BOOSTER

    Have kids hold their crosses in their hands as you lead them in a time of quiet reflection. As you read Isaiah 53:3-9, 11, ask kids to think of Jesus' suffering as they *gently* press the tips of the twigs into the palms of their hands. Close with a prayer, thanking Jesus that he loved enough to die for us and that he lives to be our Savior.

SUPPLIES

- ❏ leather shoelaces
- ❏ jute twine
- ❏ wild bird feathers or craft feathers
- ❏ small twigs
- ❏ craft glue

PRO POINTER

You may want to photocopy the handout on page 57 if you have a lot of kids who need help with square knots.

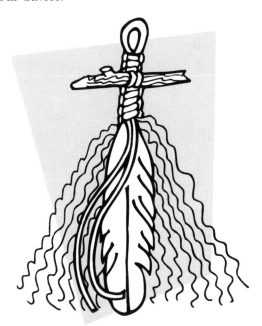

AUTOGRAPH SHIRTS

"Only those whose names are written in the Lamb's book of life will enter the city"(Revelation 21:27b).

SUPPLIES

- ❑ prewashed cotton T-shirts
- ❑ clean cardboard
- ❑ clip-style clothespins
- ❑ permanent markers

PRO POINTER

Be sure to create a shirt for yourself; kids will enjoy signing it, and a few years down the road it will be a museum piece!

This autograph craft is a great friendship builder! Use it as you open a year with a new group of kids, or as a souvenir of a special event.

1. Give each child a T-shirt, a sheet of cardboard that fits snugly inside the T-shirt, and four clothespins.

2. Demonstrate how to stretch the front and back of a T-shirt so it's flat and smooth across the cardboard. Gather and clip the extra width of T-shirt with clothespins at all four corners of the cardboard.

3. Have kids use permanent markers to write their names on the fronts of their shirts in big letters—as plain or fancy as they please.

4. Turn kids loose for an autograph party with these two guidelines: everyone signs everyone else's shirt, and all comments written with the autographs are positive and encouraging.

FAITH BOOSTER

Ask:

● **Where would you like your name to be written someday? on the license plate of your very own car? on the cover of a book you've written? In a Hall of Fame? in newspaper headlines? on the door of the Oval Office of the White House? on a check for a million dollars?**

Encourage several children to respond. Explain that it would be nice to have your name in all those places, but in the end, there's only one place where it really counts. Have children listen for that place as you read Revelation 21:27 aloud. Ask:

● **How can you know that your name is written there?**

Take this opportunity to explain how your kids can know that Jesus has forgiven their sins and written their names in the book of life.

SOCK-IN-THE-MOUTH PUPPETS

"I hope my words and thoughts please you. Lord, you are my Rock, the one who saves me" (Psalm 19:14).

● ●

Here's a new twist on the good ole sock puppet that's as cute as can be.

1. Before craft time, recruit an assistant with a sewing machine or one who is handy with a needle and thread.

2. Let kids each choose a sock and a color of felt. Show kids how to lay the toes of the sock on the felt and then trace around them. Help kids cut around the edge of the toes, as shown in the illustration below. Then have them fold the felt and cut around the tracing.

4. Have your sewing assistant slip the folded felt inside the open toes, pin the top and bottom of the felt to the top and bottom of the toes, and top-stitch the felt in place. Now the puppets have nice working mouths!

5. Encourage kids to use imagination as they add eyes and other features by gluing buttons, yarn, and felt onto their puppets.

FAITH BOOSTER

Gather kids and ask to hear what their finished puppets have to say. After several puppets have "responded," ask:

● **How did you decide what your puppets were going to say?**
● **What do your puppets' words tell us about them?**
● **Who puts the words in your mouth?**
● **What do your words say about you?**

Ask kids to listen to what King David said about his words; then read Psalm 19:14 aloud. Write "always," "sometimes," and "never" on three separate sheets of paper, and lay them on the floor a few feet apart. Ask kids to stand by the paper that reflects how often their words are pleasing to God. Encourage kids to be the "masters of their mouths," and please God with their words.

SUPPLIES

❏ assorted socks
❏ red, green, brown, and yellow felt
❏ scissors
❏ straight pins
❏ assorted buttons
❏ yarn
❏ craft glue
❏ sewing machine or needle and thread
❏ markers

PRO POINTER

Encourage your sewing assistant to ease and scrunch the sock fabric to make it fit around the felt—perfect tailoring is not necessary!

FRIENDSHIP BRACELETS

"A friend loves you all the time, and a brother helps in time of trouble" (Proverbs 17:17).

Simple square knots produce beautiful results! These colorful bracelets are perennial favorites with kids.

1. Before craft time, cut several skeins of embroidery floss into thirty-inch strands. Each strand of embroidery floss contains six separate threads. Keep the floss intact; don't separate the threads.

2. Let each student choose two strands of two different colors of floss. Demonstrate how to tie all four strands together at one end in an overhand knot. Have kids tape the tied end to the edge of a table.

3. Arrange the two strands of color A in the middle and the two strands of color B on the outside.

4. Tie three square knots with color B. Then pull color B to the inside and color A to the outside.

5. Tie three square knots with color A. Then pull color A to the inside and color B to the outside. Continue alternating square knots of the two colors until the bracelet is the desired length.

6. Untie the overhand knot at the top of the bracelet. Tie the top and bottom of the bracelet together in one large overhand knot. Trim the ends so you leave a two- to three-inch tail.

SUPPLIES

- ❑ scissors
- ❑ embroidery floss
- ❑ tape

PRO POINTER

Be sure to purchase floss in "guy colors" such as black, turquoise, red, burgundy, and forest green.

FAITH BOOSTER

Ask:

- ● **Why are these called "friendship bracelets"?**
- ● **What's important to you in a friend?**

Read Proverbs 17:17 aloud, and ask kids to explain the verse in their own words. Then form groups of six kids. The kids in each group need to be approximately the same size. With one group at a time, have a volunteer stand in the center as you make a tight circle by locking elbows with five kids. Tell the volunteer to close his or her eyes, keep his or her body rigid, and fall back against the circle. Because the people in the circle are standing close together with their elbows locked, they can easily hold the weight of the volunteer. Repeat with other volunteers. Then ask:

- ● **What was it like to catch someone?**
- ● **Why were your willing to close your eyes and let yourself fall?**
- ● **How is that like the trust you feel in your friendships?**
- ● **What makes you trust someone?**

Encourage kids to be "trustable" friends.

FAITHFUL FRIDGE FRIENDS

"Be careful. Don't think these little children are worth nothing. I tell you that they have angels in heaven who are always with my Father in heaven" (Matthew 18:10).

SUPPLIES

- ❑ scissors
- ❑ clean nylon hose
- ❑ needles and thread
- ❑ three-inch wide lace
- ❑ polyester fiber stuffing
- ❑ fine-point permanent black markers
- ❑ foil garland of stars
- ❑ craft glue or hot glue gun
- ❑ cardboard circles
- ❑ self-adhesive magnets

These angelic creations will remind kids that God's faithful guardians are always with them.

1. Before craft time, cut off the legs from nylon hose, cut all the way up the legs, and lay the fabric flat. Cut five-inch circles from the fabric. Thread one needle for each child and knot the thread at the end. Cut the lace into four-inch strips.

2. Give each child a circle of nylon fabric, a threaded needle, and a ball of stuffing. Demonstrate how to sew loose stitches around the edge of the circle, place the stuffing in the center of the circle, and then pull the thread tight behind the ball of stuffing, knot it, and leave the excess thread hanging.

3. Tell kids that the smooth side of the ball is the angel's face. Have kids flatten it a little and then use a fine-point marker to draw two circles for eyes.

4. Give each child a strip of lace. Have kids pinch the lace in the center, wrap the excess thread around the gathered center, then stitch or glue the lace to the backs of the head to form wings. Help kids knot and trim their thread.

5. To form a halo, let each person cut a small strip of foil garland, twist it into a circle with a small tail, and glue the tail to the back of the head at the top.

6. Help kids glue the angels' heads to two-inch cardboard circles. For best results, have an adult use a hot glue gun.

7. Have kids attach a self-adhesive magnet to the back of the cardboard circle.

PRO POINTER

Kids who have never used needle and thread can easily complete this project. Just warn kids to be careful of the needles' sharp points. The stitches around the fabric circle can be very loose and awkward since they are simply gathered to pull the circle into a ball.

FAITH BOOSTER

Ask:

● **Who can tell about a time God protected you?**

Read Matthew 18:10 aloud, then ask:

● **How does it make you feel to know that God has special angels who watch over you?**

Encourage kids to discuss what they know about angels from the Bible. Be prepared to correct any misconceptions kids might have developed from secular views about angels. Explain that they are mighty messengers from God, that they can fight great battles, and that they protect God's people. Make sure children understand that angels take their orders from God and that we don't worship angels—we worship the God who created them.

Encourage kids to put their angels on the refrigerator as a reminder of God's loving protection.

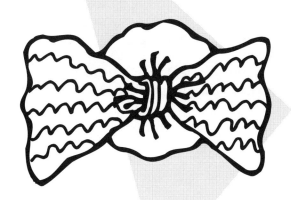

FLEECY LAMBS

"The Lord is my shepherd; I have everything I need" (Psalm 23:1).

● ● ● ● ● ● ● ● ● ● ● ● ● ● ● ● ● ● ● ●

SUPPLIES

❏ fleece
❏ black felt
❏ scissors
❏ poster board
❏ craft glue or a hot glue gun
❏ optional: wiggly eyes

PRO POINTER

Plush terry cloth makes a good substitute for fleece.

These cute little guys are a great project for Christmas, Easter, or any time, and they'll serve as great reminders that Jesus is our shepherd.

1. Before craft time, photocopy the fleecy lamb patterns (p.61), and trace them onto poster board.

2. Have kids trace around the poster board patterns to cut bodies from fleece, and legs, ears, and heads from black felt.

3. Show kids how to fold the legs and glue them to the bottom inside of the bodies. Help each child glue the head to the body, then glue and press the body together.

4. Assist kids in gluing ears to both sides of the heads. Help kids add wiggly eyes if desirable.

FAITH BOOSTER

Form six groups—a group can be as small as one or two kids. Hand out Bibles, and assign each group one verse of Psalm 23. Ask kids to make up actions to tell what their verses mean. Encourage them to use their whole bodies to get the meaning across. Give kids a couple of minutes to plan, then read Psalm 23 aloud, and have each group perform its verse. Ask:

● **How does performing this psalm make you feel about Jesus?**

● **How can you use your fleecy lambs to remind you that Jesus is your shepherd?**

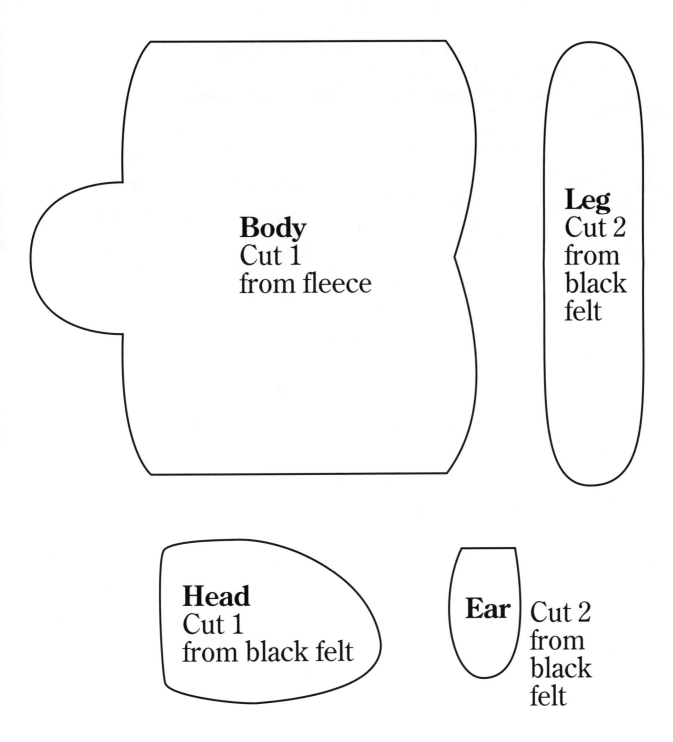

Body
Cut 1
from fleece

Leg
Cut 2
from
black
felt

Head
Cut 1
from black felt

Ear Cut 2
from
black
felt

61

TiE-DYE-RiFiC

"Just as the heavens are higher than the earth, so are my ways higher than your ways and my thoughts than your thoughts" (Isaiah 55:9).

● ● ● ● ● ● ● ● ● ● ● ● ● ● ● ● ● ● ●

SUPPLIES

- ❏ dye packet
- ❏ large stew pot
- ❏ long spoon
- ❏ rubber bands

your choice of cotton items to dye, such as

- ❏ socks
- ❏ shoelaces
- ❏ material for head-bands
- ❏ T-shirts

PRO POINTER

Cold-water dyes are available at most craft stores. They're easier to use, and you can do the whole process outside, where you won't have to worry about spills.

Tie-dyeing is great fun. If you've never tried it, it's time you do!

1. Let kids know ahead of time to wear old clothes.

2. In a large stew pot, use a long spoon to mix the dye bath according to directions given with the dye.

3. To make a random pattern, let kids wad up their items and wrap them with rubber bands going in every direction.

4. To make striped patterns, show kids how to fold or roll the items and wrap them with rubber bands every couple of inches.

5. Help kids dye the cloth according to the directions on the package of dye.

6. Rinse the items well in cold water. Then have kids remove all the rubber bands and rinse the items again.

7. Have kids smooth out the items and let them dry in the sun. Or, give kids plastic bags for carrying their items home. Be sure kids know that their dyed items should be washed separately for the first few times.

FAITH BOOSTER

Ask:

● **What did you think your project would look like?**

● **Did it come out the way you thought it would?**

Say: **We never know exactly what's going to happen in our lives. Sometimes great things happen—like when a parent gets a raise, or your team wins a championship. Sometimes hard things happen, like when someone you love gets very sick, you lose a pet, or your parents split up. When those things happen, it may feel like your life doesn't make sense at all—like it's as crazy as the patterns we dyed! But the Bible says not to worry, that God has things under control.**

Read Isaiah 55:9 aloud. Ask:

● **What does that verse mean to you?**

● **How can we trust God when our lives seem out of control?**

Explain that Scripture tells us that God even knows how many hairs are on our head. We can trust him in good times and bad. And, like our designs, we know things will come out beautiful in the end when we trust God.

DENIM PRAYER RUGS

"Do not worry about anything, but pray and ask God for everything you need, always giving thanks" (Philippians 4:6).

● ● ● ● ● ● ● ● ● ● ● ● ● ● ● ●

These soft, colorful rugs will encourage children to set aside a special place and time to pray.

1. If your denim fabric is forty-five inches wide, cut twenty-two-by-eighteen-inch rectangles to get four rugs from one yard. If your fabric is sixty inches wide, cut twenty-by-eighteen-inch rectangles to get six rugs from one yard.

2. On a sewing machine, run a quick straight stitch around each rectangle, one-half inch in from the edge. Then wash and dry the rectangles, and you'll have nice, fluffy frayed edges.

3. Begin by doing the Faith Booster below.

4. Set out the fabric paint pens, slick fabric paint, and craft jewels. Encourage kids to write messages such as, "Take time to pray," "Trust God," or, "Give thanks" on their rugs; then have kids embellish the corners by gluing on a few jewels.

5. Set the rugs in a sunny place to dry.

SUPPLIES

❑ denim fabric
❑ sewing machine
❑ fabric paint pens
❑ slick fabric paint
❑ craft "jewels"
❑ washer and dryer
❑ glue

FAITH BOOSTER

Ask:
● **Who remembers the story of Daniel in the lion's den?**
● **Who can tell me how Daniel ended up in the lion's den?**
● **Why did he keep praying if it was dangerous?**
● **When do you pray?**

Read Philippians 4:6-7 aloud. Ask:
● **Why does God want us to pray?**
● **What happens when we pray?**

Say: **It's important to pray every day, and sometimes it's helpful to have a special time and place to pray.** Explain that the kids are going to make prayer rugs, but they don't have to kneel on them. They might like to keep their rugs with their Bibles and spread the rugs on their laps or on the bed beside them as they pray. Or they might drape them on the back of a chair as a reminder to pray.

FRIDGE FLOWERS

"The grass dies and the flowers fall, but the word of our God will live forever" (Isaiah 40:8).

SUPPLIES

- ❑ paper
- ❑ poster board patterns
- ❑ markers
- ❑ scissors
- ❑ fabric scraps
- ❑ assorted buttons
- ❑ needles and thread
  or a hot glue gun
- ❑ self-adhesive magnets

Bright and sweet, these little blossoms are quick to make from scraps of fabric.

1. Before craft time, draw three sizes of flower-petal patterns onto paper (see illustration below). Cut out the patterns, and trace them onto poster board. Make three or four sets of poster board patterns.

2. Have kids use markers to trace each pattern on fabric scraps. They may use the same fabric or contrasting ones.

3. Demonstrate how to place the largest petal on the bottom, the medium petal in the middle, and the smallest petal on top.

4. Have kids each choose a button, and show them how to center the button on the top petal. Then let kids sew the buttons to the petals, starting from behind the largest petal. Or, have an adult use a hot glue gun to help kids glue their flowers together.

5. Have kids knot and tie off the thread and stick a self-adhesive magnet to the back of the flower.

FAITH BOOSTER

Tell kids you're going to have some fun exploring the life of a flower. Have them be a "packet of seeds" by curling up into little balls and huddling together. Then have them "bloom" by lying in a circle with their feet pointed to the middle and their arms stretched out in a Y overhead. Then say that it's one hundred degrees, and they haven't been watered in a week. After kids have "wilted," gather them in a circle, and ask:

- ● **How long do flowers usually last?**

Explain that the prophet Isaiah compared people to flowers. Read Isaiah 40:6-8. Ask:

- ● **How are people like flowers and grass?**
- ● **What lasts forever?**

Encourage kids to base their lives on God's Word, which lasts forever.

PRO POINTER

These fabric posies also make great decorations for hats, vests, place mats, bulletin boards, and packages. At Christmas, make them in red and green!

OJOS DE DIOS

"Two sparrows cost only a penny, but not even one of them can die without your Father's knowing it. God even knows how many hairs are on your head. So don't be afraid. You are worth much more than many sparrows" (Matthew 10:29-31).

● ●

Popular in Mexico and the Southwest, these simple weavings can be made in beautiful colors to complement every season.

1. You may use dowels of any length or thickness. For beginners, a good size is quarter-inch dowels about six or eight inches long.

2. Show kids how to cross the dowels in the middle and wrap them diagonally twice in both directions as shown in the diagram below.

3. Demonstrate how to wrap the yarn over the next arm and then around it, over the next arm and then around it, and so on, as shown below.

4. Kids may use as many colors of yarn as they'd like. To change colors of yarn, tuck the yarn ends into the part that's already been completed.

5. When the arms are full, have kids tuck the yarn end behind one of the arms and secure it with glue.

SUPPLIES

- ❏ dowels, chopsticks, craft sticks, or twigs
- ❏ different colors of yarn
- ❏ glue

FAITH BOOSTER

Explain that the name "Ojo de Dios" (O-ho day dee-OSE) means "God's eye." Tell kids that while some cultures may use them as good luck charms, we know that they're just pretty decorations and reminders that God is always watching over us. Ask kids to listen to what Jesus said about how God watches over us. Read Matthew 10:29-30 aloud. Then have kids form pairs, and give partners one minute each to see how many hairs they can count on each other's heads.

Ask:

● **What do these verses tell you about how much God cares for you?**

Challenge kids to share these verses with their families when they take home their ojos.

PRO POINTER

It's fine to use yarns of different weights and textures. Empty your scrap barrel, and see what happens!

BANDANNA TREASURE POCKETS

"Your heart will be where your treasure is" (Luke 12:34).

● ● ● ● ● ● ● ● ● ● ● ● ● ● ● ●

SUPPLIES

❑ bandannas or squares of fabric
❑ safety pins
❑ poster board
❑ scissors
❑ glue

These nifty treasure pockets can be made in a jiffy from any kind of cloth—and they're good for holding everything from peanuts to pencils!

1. Have kids fold their squares of fabric in quarters and lay them down with the four loose points at the top.

2. Demonstrate how to take the two top points and roll them down to the center as shown below.

3. Instruct kids to flip over their fabric. Fold the left and right points to the center and secure them with a safety pin.

4. Have kids turn over their fabric. Let them each cut a piece of poster board to slip between the two bottom layers and stiffen the pocket. Have each kid stick the tips of the fabric to the poster board with a dot of glue.

FAITH BOOSTER

Ask kids what kinds of things they'll keep in their treasure pockets. Then read aloud Luke 12:32-34. Ask:

● **Why does Jesus want us to be generous with people who have less than we do?**

● **What does it mean when Jesus says that our hearts will be where our treasure is?**

● **What kind of treasure will we have in heaven?**

Talk about how easy it is to want more things. Encourage kids to think of those who have less than they do.

PRO POINTER

This craft is based on a napkin folding technique. Use it the next time you entertain, and place silverware in the pocket.

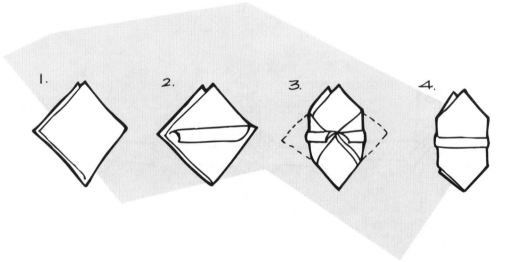

LITTLEST ANGELS

"The angel came to her and said, 'Greetings! The Lord has blessed you and is with you'" (Luke 1:28).

● ●

Quick and easy to assemble, these adorable angels make great Christmas decorations.

1. Before craft time, use pinking shears to cut muslin into eight-inch circles. Cut jute twine into eight-inch lengths. Cut lace into four-inch lengths.

2. Give each child a muslin circle, a cotton ball, a length of jute twine, and a piece of lace.

3. Demonstrate how to place a cotton ball in the center of the circle, gather the muslin around it, and tie the twine just beneath the cotton ball to form a head and neck. Knot the twine behind the head.

4. Show kids how to pinch the lace in the center and tie the twine around it to form wings.

5. Let kids take a bit of Spanish moss, pull it into halo shapes, and glue the halos to the top of the heads. You may want to have an adult do the gluing with a hot glue gun.

6. If you wish, let kids glue tiny dried flowers to the halos.

FAITH BOOSTER

Have kids sit in a group with their backs to you, and be ready to catch whatever you throw in their direction. Kids may not turn around to see what's coming. Toss a soft foam ball a few times so several kids have an opportunity to catch it. Then gather kids in a circle and read aloud Luke 1:26-38. Ask:

● **How was our game like what happened to Mary?**

● **Do you think Mary was expecting a visit from an angel that day? Why or why not?**

Explain that God used ordinary people to bring his Son into the world. They didn't know what God had in store for them, but they were willing and obedient when the time came. Say that God can still use ordinary people to accomplish great things. Encourage kids to be open to God's plans.

SUPPLIES

- [ ] *unbleached muslin*
- [ ] *pinking shears*
- [ ] *jute twine*
- [ ] *two-inch wide beige lace*
- [ ] *cotton balls*
- [ ] *Spanish moss*
- [ ] *craft glue or hot glue gun*
- [ ] *optional: tiny dried flowers*

PRO POINTER

As an alternative to lace, make simple wings by looping jute twine back and forth several times, then tying the loops in the middle.

BACK

BEAUTEMOUS BOTANICALS

CLAY IMPRESSIONS

"We have this treasure from God, but we are like clay jars that hold the treasure. This shows that the great power is from God, not from us" (2 Corinthians 4:7).

● ●

Pressing leaves or sprigs of pine into self-hardening clay brings beautiful results.

1. Show kids how to place a small lump of clay between layers of wax paper. Use a rolling pin or pop can to roll it fairly thin.

2. Let kids lay leaves or sprigs of pine under the top layer of their wax paper and press the leaves into the clay with rolling pins.

3. Demonstrate how to carefully lift the wax paper and then lift the leaves or sprigs off the clay. Kids can uses pencils to make holes in the top of the plaques and lay the plaques in the sun to dry.

4. Help kids cut six-inch lengths of jute twine. When the plaques are dry, kids can thread the twine through the holes and tie them to form hangers.

FAITH BOOSTER

Compliment kids on their plaques. Ask:

● **What made these come out so beautiful?**

Help kids understand that by using items from nature, they've allowed God to be the artist. Ask them to listen to a Scripture that tells about another way we can work with God. Read 2 Corinthians 4:5-7 aloud. Ask:

● **What is the treasure these verses are talking about?**

● **How are we like clay jars?**

Explain that we're just ordinary people, but we have wonderful news to share—news about Jesus. When we let God be the artist who works in our lives, we can share that treasured news with everyone.

SUPPLIES

- ☐ self-hardening clay
- ☐ wax paper
- ☐ rolling pins or pop can
- ☐ leaves or sprigs of pine
- ☐ pencils
- ☐ jute twine

PRO POINTER

If kids are unhappy with the shape of their plaques, they can simply roll the clay back into a ball and begin again.

VANILLA BEADS

"Mary brought in a pint of very expensive perfume made from pure nard. She poured the perfume on Jesus' feet, and then she wiped his feet with her hair. And the sweet smell from the perfume filled the whole house" (John 12:3).

● ●

SUPPLIES

☐ vanilla potpourri
☐ resealable plastic bags
☐ pop cans
☐ flour
☐ salt
☐ vanilla
☐ water
☐ measuring spoons
☐ mixing bowls
☐ round toothpicks
☐ microwave oven
☐ metallic thread
☐ optional: bay leaves, dried rose buds, olive oil

The pleasant, neutral scent of vanilla makes these little balls of fragrance suitable for guys or girls.

1. Form groups of six. Instruct three kids from each group to place one cup of vanilla potpourri in resealable plastic bags, seal the bags, and crush the potpourri by using pop cans like a rolling pin.

2. Have the other three kids from each group mix a dough using the following proportions: one-half cup of flour, one teaspoon of salt, one teaspoon of vanilla, and two tablespoons of water.

3. Let kids mix the crushed potpourri with the dough and take turns kneading the mixture. Help kids adjust the dough by adding more flour or water to achieve a smooth consistency.

4. Have each child take a ball of dough, roll it into beads, and pierce the beads with a round toothpick.

5. Dry the beads for several minutes in a microwave oven set on half power.

6. Let kids string the beads on metallic thread. If you wish, let guys add two or three bay leaves to their string and let girls add two or three dried rose buds.

FAITH BOOSTER

Explain to kids that they can place vanilla beads in a drawer, hang them in a closet, or hang them as a wall decoration. Tell kids that oils and perfumes were extremely expensive in biblical times, and say that one woman gave Jesus a gift of expensive perfume. Read aloud John 12:1-3. Ask:

● **How did this gift show Mary's love for Jesus?**
● **How do you show your love for Jesus?**

Encourage kids to let their vanilla beads remind them to show their love for Jesus every day.

PRO POINTER

Since there are so many types of potpourri on the market, it's hard to predict the texture of the dough. If it seems too crumbly, try adding a bit of olive oil.

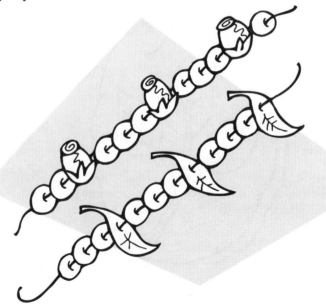

FLORAL FRAMES

"The Lord is all I need. He takes care of me. My share in life has been pleasant; my part has been beautiful" (Psalm 16:5-6).

● ● ● ● ● ● ● ● ● ● ● ● ● ● ● ●

Simple materials and easy gluing result in a beautiful frame.

1. Give each child a wooden frame. Set out a pile of Spanish moss, and show kids how to separate and spread it into thin lines.

2. Have kids run a line of glue down one side of their wooden frames, then press the moss into the glue. Encourage them to use plenty of moss so the frames don't show through. Have kids repeat this with the other three sides.

3. Let kids choose dried flowers and glue them to the moss here and there around the frames.

4. If you wish, take instant-print pictures of the kids, and let them slide the pictures into their finished frames.

FAITH BOOSTER

Observe that whoever gets "framed" with this craft will be surrounded by beautiful things—like standing in a meadow of flowers. Point out that King David appreciated the beautiful life God had given him. Read Psalm 16:5-6 aloud. Then ask:

● **How has God made your life pleasant?**

● **What beautiful places has God shown to you?**

Show children pictures of beautiful mountains, oceans, or other natural scenery. Encourage children to recognize and be thankful for all the beauty and pleasant things God has put in our lives.

SUPPLIES

❑ *Spanish moss*

❑ *small, inexpensive wooden picture frames*

❑ *craft glue or hot glue gun*

❑ *assorted dried flowers*

❑ *optional: instant-print camera*

PRO POINTER

To save the expense of buying frames, you may wish to make cardboard frames according to the instructions from the "Twig Frames" activity (p. 16).

RAFFIA BOWS

"Look at the birds. They don't plant or harvest, they don't have storerooms or barns, but God feeds them. And you are worth much more than birds" (Luke 12:24).

●●●●●●●●●●●●●●●●●●●●●●●●●

SUPPLIES

- ❑ photocopies of the "Luke 12:24" handout
- ❑ scissors
- ❑ parchment
- ❑ raffia
- ❑ craft glue or hot glue gun
- ❑ craft birds
- ❑ tiny dried flowers
- ❑ hole punch
- ❑ jute twine

These lovely wall or door decorations are simple to make from natural materials.

1. Before craft time, make copies of the "Luke 12:24" verses (p. 73) onto parchment or card stock. Cut apart the verses and give each child one copy of the verse.

2. Give each child enough strands of raffia to tie a nice, full bow. Help kids tie the raffia into a bow.

3. Have each child glue around the front and back of the bow so it cannot come untied.

4. Let each child choose a craft bird and glue it to the center of the bow, then glue a few dried flowers around the bird.

5. Have each child take the handout, punch a hole in one end, loop a length of jute twine through the hole and around the center of the bow and tie.

FAITH BOOSTER

Ask:

● **Have you ever seen a bird that looked worried?**

● **What kinds of hardships do wild birds face?**

● **If birds have to find their food in the wild and face all kinds of predators such as cats, why aren't they worried?**

Have kids read the verses they attached to their bows. Ask:

● **If birds don't worry, who do they trust to take care of them?**

● **Is it easy or hard for you to trust God to take care of you? Explain.**

Encourage kids to read the verse on their raffia bows when they're feeling worried.

PRO POINTER

Some brands of potpourri contain small dried flowers. The fragrance from the flowers makes a welcome addition to the beauty of this craft.

Look at the birds. They don't plant or harvest, they don't have storerooms or barns, but God feeds them. And you are worth much more than birds (Luke 12:24).

Look at the birds. They don't plant or harvest, they don't have storerooms or barns, but God feeds them. And you are worth much more than birds (Luke 12:24).

Look at the birds. They don't plant or harvest, they don't have storerooms or barns, but God feeds them. And you are worth much more than birds (Luke 12:24).

Look at the birds. They don't plant or harvest, they don't have storerooms or barns, but God feeds them. And you are worth much more than birds (Luke 12:24).

Look at the birds. They don't plant or harvest, they don't have storerooms or barns, but God feeds them. And you are worth much more than birds (Luke 12:24).

Look at the birds. They don't plant or harvest, they don't have storerooms or barns, but God feeds them. And you are worth much more than birds (Luke 12:24).

Look at the birds. They don't plant or harvest, they don't have storerooms or barns, but God feeds them. And you are worth much more than birds (Luke 12:24).

Look at the birds. They don't plant or harvest, they don't have storerooms or barns, but God feeds them. And you are worth much more than birds (Luke 12:24).

Look at the birds. They don't plant or harvest, they don't have storerooms or barns, but God feeds them. And you are worth much more than birds (Luke 12:24).

Look at the birds. They don't plant or harvest, they don't have storerooms or barns, but God feeds them. And you are worth much more than birds (Luke 12:24).

Look at the birds. They don't plant or harvest, they don't have storerooms or barns, but God feeds them. And you are worth much more than birds (Luke 12:24).

CORNHUSK CRÈCHES

"While they were in Bethlehem, the time came for Mary to have the baby, and she gave birth to her first son. Because there were no rooms left in the inn, she wrapped the baby with pieces of cloth and laid him in a box where animals are fed" (Luke 2:6-7).

● ●

SUPPLIES

- ❑ dried cornhusks
- ❑ bucket of warm water
- ❑ paper clips
- ❑ plastic foam cups
- ❑ pins
- ❑ heavy wire
- ❑ optional: small straw wreaths, greenery, and a star

Pioneer children played with cornhusk dolls. Now your kids can make these traditional toys into a charming crèche scene.

1. Soak cornhusks in warm water. Have children watch you make a complete doll before they begin making their own.

2. To make Mary, select about eight cornhusks and tie them together about an inch from the top. Tear off a strip of cornhusk to use as string.

3. To make the head, hold the short ends in one hand and turn each long cornhusk down so that the short ends are hidden inside. Use a strip of cornhusk to tie a neck.

4. To make arms, roll three cornhusks together. Tie wrists at each end. Trim the hands so they're even.

5. To insert the arms, separate the eight cornhusks just below the neck. Slide the arms in place, and tie a waist. Bring the hands to the front, and clip them with a paper clip.

6. Bend the doll into a sitting position and pin it to a foam cup to dry. Trim the skirts so they're even.

7. Make a scarf by folding a large husk and tying it behind the neck.

8. Make Joseph by following steps 1 through 7. Clip husks several inches below the waist, tie ankles, and trim the feet. Tie a scarf around his forehead. Make a staff by wrapping and gluing a husk around a heavy wire. Glue the staff to Joseph's hands.

9. Make baby Jesus by folding a large husk in half twice. Roll the edges together, and tie a neck. Glue the baby in Mary's arms.

10. If you wish, lay a small straw wreath on a table and stand another wreath inside it. Place the figures on the wreaths. Add greenery to the wreaths and add a star at the top.

PRO POINTER

You can find packaged cornhusks in the Mexican food section of your grocery store. (They're used to wrap tamales!)

FAITH BOOSTER

Ask:
- **Who remembers what gifts the wise men brought to Jesus?**

Explain that we can still give gifts to Jesus and that Jesus himself told us how. Read aloud Matthew 25:31, 40, then ask:
- **How can we give gifts to Jesus?**

Give kids small scraps of Christmas gift wrap. Ask them to write on the back of the wrap one gift they'll give to Jesus and then tuck the "gift" into Mary's arms. Close with prayer, thanking Jesus for the gift of himself.

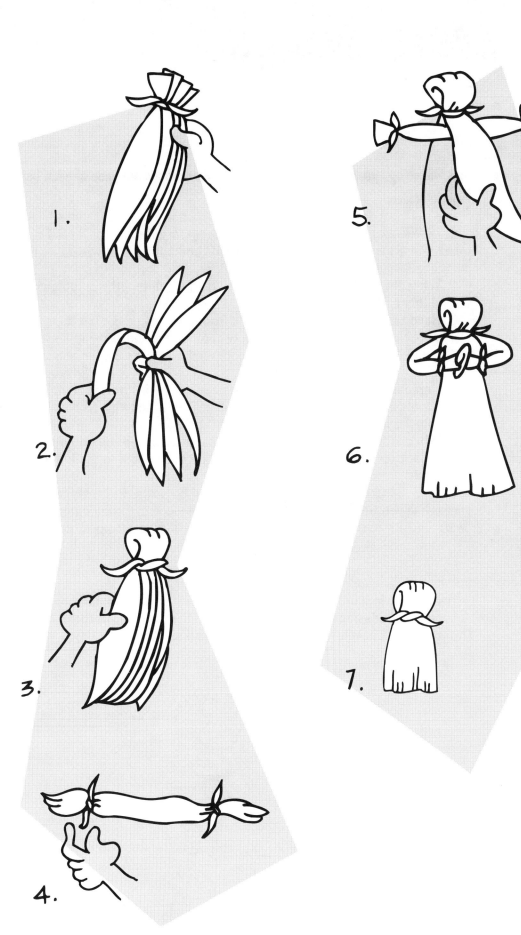

1.

2.

3.

4.

5.

6.

7.

APPLE SWAGS

"You give the year a good harvest, and you load the wagons with many crops" (Psalm 65:9).

SUPPLIES

- ☐ red apples
- ☐ paring knives
- ☐ lemon juice
- ☐ clean bucket
- ☐ water
- ☐ scissors
- ☐ jute twine
- ☐ tapestry needles
- ☐ towels
- ☐ bay leaves
- ☐ cinnamon potpourri oil

Kids will enjoy making these fragrant, festive decorations any time of year, but fall is especially nice.

1. Let kids wash the apples. Help kids *carefully* cut the apples vertically into quarter-inch slices and then drop the slices into a bucket of water to which you've added half a cup of lemon juice.

2. While the apples soak, help kids cut thirty-inch lengths of jute twine and thread them onto tapestry needles.

3. Have kids remove the apple slices from the bucket and pat them dry with towels. Let each child take fifteen to twenty apple slices and several bay leaves.

4. Let kids put drops of cinnamon potpourri oil on the center of five or six apple slices.

5. Demonstrate how to poke the tapestry needles just to the right of the center of the apple slices and thread the apple slices onto the twine. Have kids add two or three bay leaves between every five or six apple slices.

6. When kids string all their slices and bay leaves, demonstrate how to run the thread back up through the slices, poking the needle just to the left of the center of each slice.

7. Help kids even their twine at the top and tie bows. Kids may hang the apple slices to dry in the open air, or ask a parent to place the swag in an oven set on "warm" to dry overnight. The apples will keep their spicy smell after they've dried!

FAITH BOOSTER

Ask kids to join in an alphabet harvest prayer. Say, "Dear Lord, we thank you for A," and have kids name fruits and vegetables that begin with that letter. Continue through the alphabet, then have everyone shout, "Amen!"

PRO POINTER

You'll find bay leaves in the spice section of your grocery store.

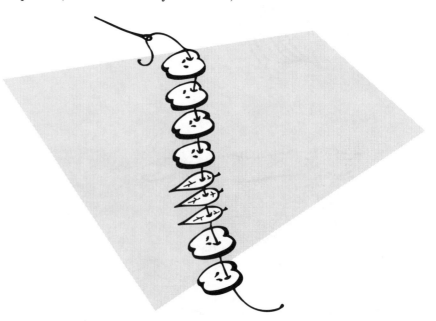

APPLE-DAPPLE WREATHS

"The Lord God caused every beautiful tree and every tree that was good for food to grow out of the ground" (Genesis 2:9a).

● ● ● ● ● ● ● ● ● ● ● ● ● ● ● ●

Wreaths are a sign of joy and celebration. Kids will be proud of these "fruitful" creations!

1. Before craft time, prepare a twelve-inch circle of cardboard for each child. Cut a five-inch circle from the center of each cardboard piece.

2. Let kids wash the apples. Help kids *carefully* cut the apples vertically into quarter-inch slices and drop the slices into a bucket of water to which you've added a half-cup of lemon juice.

3. Have kids remove the apple slices from the bucket and pat them dry with towels.

4. Spread the apple slices in a microwave oven and run the oven at half power for ten minutes. It's not necessary for the apple slices to dry completely; they will continue to air dry when they're placed on the wreaths.

5. As the apples are drying, have kids punch two holes in the top of their wreaths and tie lengths of ribbon through the holes to make hangers.

6. Have kids smear their cardboard rings with craft glue and press Spanish moss into the glue.

7. Let kids glue cooled apple slices around their wreaths. You may want to provide cinnamon sticks, tiny pine cones, and bay leaves to further decorate the wreaths.

8. Remind kids to keep their wreaths flat until the glue has dried.

FAITH BOOSTER

Gather kids in the shade of a tree. Ask:
● **When are trees first mentioned in the Bible?**
Read aloud Genesis 2:8-9, 15. Ask:
● **What job did God give Adam?**
● **What are some of the things trees provide for us?**
Explain that the job of caring for the trees that God gave Adam has passed on to us. Talk about how a tree can benefit generations of people. Challenge kids to be caretakers of trees. You may want to get permission to plant a small seedling on your church property. Close by giving the tree you're near a group hug!

SUPPLIES

- ❏ cardboard
- ❏ scissors
- ❏ red apples
- ❏ lemon juice
- ❏ water
- ❏ clean bucket
- ❏ towels
- ❏ microwave oven
- ❏ hole punch
- ❏ ribbon
- ❏ Spanish moss
- ❏ craft glue
- ❏ optional: cinnamon sticks, tiny pine cones, and bay leaves

PRO POINTER

Red Delicious apples are particularly nice for this craft because of their heart-shaped slices.

LEAF PRINT PLACE MATS

"So you will go out with joy and be led out in peace. The mountains and hills will burst into song before you, and all the trees in the fields will clap their hands" (Isaiah 55:12).

● ●

SUPPLIES

- ❑ *unbleached muslin*
- ❑ *scissors*
- ❑ *fabric paint or dye*
- ❑ *a variety of leaves*
- ❑ *brushes*
- ❑ *cans of pop*
- ❑ *newspaper*

These simple creations bring the beauty of God's creation to the table.

1. Before craft time, cut ten-by-fifteen-inch place mats from unbleached muslin. You'll need one place mat for each child. Set out three or four colors of fabric paint or dye.

2. Take kids on a short hike. Have them collect three to five leaves of different sizes and shapes.

3. Let kids arrange their leaves on their place mats in a pleasing pattern.

4. Demonstrate how to brush paint onto the "ribbed" side of a leaf, press the leaf onto a place mat, roll a can of pop over it to make a clear print, then carefully lift the leaf.

5. Set the place mats in a sunny place to dry.

FAITH BOOSTER

Read aloud Isaiah 55:12. Ask:

● **Have you ever seen leaves "clap their hands" in autumn? What is that like?**

Announce that you're going to lead kids out "with joy." Explain that they must do exactly what you do. Lead the kids in a fun, celebratory game of Follow the Leader. Skip and wave your arms, sing a favorite chorus at the top of your voice, spin around, run up and down stairs, do a somersault, and generally surprise your kids with fun actions. (Just keep your heart rate at a safe training level!) Then call everyone together, take several deep breaths, and sit down. Ask:

● **What are some things that give us a reason to celebrate every day?**

Encourage kids to use their place mats as reminders to celebrate God's promise of loving care.

PRO POINTER

If you have a kind-hearted person in your church who owns a serger, he or she could quickly stitch a rolled hem around the place mats.

EGG CARTON GARDENS

"I tell you the truth, if your faith is as big as a mustard seed, you can say to this mountain, 'Move from here to there,' and it will move. All things will be possible for you" (Matthew 17:20b).

● ●

Make these mini-greenhouses on a drab winter day and you'll see hopes of spring "sprout" before your very eyes!

1. Before craft time, collect several plastic foam egg cartons. Cut them in half so each child will have six "wells."

2. Cover your work area with newspaper, then have kids spoon potting soil into each well.

3. Demonstrate how to sprinkle a few seeds on the soil and then gently press the seeds into the soil.

4. Have kids water their seeds and cover the egg cartons loosely with plastic wrap.

5. Instruct kids to keep their "gardens" moist and in a sunny spot. Have them remove the plastic wrap as soon as little shoots begin to appear.

FAITH BOOSTER

Ask kids to put a seed in their hands and follow you outside. Carry a Bible with you, and gather kids around a large tree or bush. Read Matthew 17:20b aloud and ask:

● **What is faith?**
● **How do we know if we have faith in Jesus?**
● **How can we help our faith grow?**

Encourage kids to pray for their faith to grow as their seeds grow.

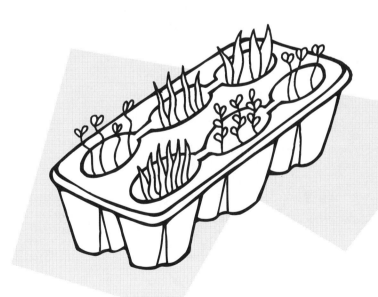

SUPPLIES

❑ *plastic foam egg cartons*
❑ *newspaper*
❑ *potting soil*
❑ *plastic spoons*
❑ *flower seeds*
❑ *plastic wrap*

PRO POINTER

Marigold and zinnia seeds are good choices because they're easy to grow. Morning glories come up quickly, too, but be sure to follow package directions for nicking them with a knife and soaking them in warm water overnight.

GRASS EGGHEADS

"God put everything under his power and made him the head over everything for the church" (Ephesians 1:22a).

● ● ● ● ● ● ● ● ● ● ● ● ● ● ● ● ●

These eggheads are very funny-looking little guys. Your kids will be delighted with them.

1. Show kids how to carefully tap around the top of an egg with a table knife, remove the top section of shell, and pour the contents into a mixing bowl.

2. Help kids rinse and dry their eggs, then have kids use fine-point permanent markers to draw interesting faces on them.

3. Have kids use plastic spoons to carefully fill the shells with potting soil to within half an inch of the top.

4. Let kids take a few seeds, gently press them into the potting soil, and water them.

5. Keep the eggheads in a warm, sunny place. The seed packages will tell how soon the seeds will sprout. Within about two weeks, the eggheads should have hilarious heads of hair!

SUPPLIES

- ❑ uncooked eggs
- ❑ table knives
- ❑ mixing bowl
- ❑ paper towels
- ❑ fine-point permanent markers
- ❑ plastic spoons
- ❑ potting soil
- ❑ grass or bean seeds
- ❑ water

FAITH BOOSTER

Tap a child on the head and ask:
- ● **What's your head good for?**

Repeat the question with several kids. Talk about all the "services" the organs in our head provide for the rest of our bodies. Say that the Bible tells us that we have another head. Ask kids to listen as you read Ephesians 1:21-23. Ask:
- ● **Who is our other "head"?**
- ● **What does Jesus do for us as our head?**

Explain that Jesus is our leader who gave his life for us, and who shows us the way to God. Read Ephesians 1:19-20, and help kids understand that when they believe in Christ, God's power is at work in them. Close in prayer thanking Jesus as the leader and the head of all the people of the Church.

PRO POINTER

You may want to keep the eggheads in an egg carton in your classroom since they are fragile to transport and the soil and seeds can be easily spilled.

PRESSED FLOWER CANDLES

"Happy are the people who know how to praise you. Lord, let them live in the light of your presence" (Psalm 89:15).

● ● ● ● ● ● ● ● ● ● ● ● ● ●

Parents will have a hard time believing that their kids made these glowing works of art!

1. Give each child a candle. Let children choose one or two pressed flowers and decide where to place them on their candles. Make sure children understand that they'll need to handle the fragile flowers very carefully.

2. Demonstrate how to brush glue on the candle where a flower will be placed.

3. Gently press the flower into the glue.

4. Add leaves in the same manner.

FAITH BOOSTER

Place all the finished candles on a table. Dim the lights in the room, then let kids light their own candles. Ask:

● **How is candlelight different from electric light?**

● **Which kind of light do you prefer?**

Talk about how candlelight gives a warm, pleasant glow. Explain that the Bible talks about another kind of light. Read Psalm 89:15 aloud. Ask:

● **What is "the light of God's presence"?**

● **How can we walk in that light?**

Encourage kids to be in God's presence by reading their Bibles and praying every day, and by praising God and remembering that he is always with them.

SUPPLIES

❑ small, white pillar candles

❑ pressed flowers

❑ craft glue

❑ brushes

❑ leaves

PRO POINTER

To press flowers, place blossoms between sheets of wax paper under a heavy book. Be sure to press some small leaves, too.

PINE CONE NESTS

"Jesus said to him, 'The foxes have holes to live in, and the birds have nests, but the Son of Man has no place to rest his head'" (Matthew 8:20).

● ● ● ● ● ● ● ● ● ● ● ● ● ● ● ● ● ● ● ●

SUPPLIES

- ❏ pine cones
- ❏ craft birds
- ❏ ribbon
- ❏ craft glue or a hot glue gun
- ❏ Spanish moss
- ❏ optional: silk blossoms or dried flowers, greenery, or glitter glue

These natural beauties are quick to make and can be "customized" for every season!

1. Let kids choose a pine cone, a craft bird, and ribbon. Cut the ribbon into fifteen-inch lengths.

2. Have kids hold their pine cones with the wide ends at the top. Help kids put glue on the wide end of the pine cone and press Spanish moss into the glue to form a nest. Let them each glue a craft bird in the nest.

3. Help kids run a line of glue between the first and second row of petals of the pine cone. Have kids wrap a ribbon around the glue-line twice so you end up with the ends of the ribbon on opposite sides of the pine cone. Let kids tie the ribbon into a bow to form a hanger.

FAITH BOOSTER

Ask:

● **When Jesus was on earth, where did he live?**

Explain that Jesus grew up in Nazareth and that Joseph, his earthly father, was a carpenter. But after Jesus started to preach, he went from town to town and stayed in his followers' homes. Ask:

● **What are some of the miracles Jesus did?**

● **What do you think people did after they saw those miracles?**

Say that many people who saw Jesus' miracles wanted to follow him. Ask kids to listen to what Jesus told them, then read Matthew 8:20. Ask:

● **What was Jesus trying to say?**

Explain that Jesus wanted to let people know that following him wouldn't be easy. He gave up things that are important to people—like having a comfortable home—so he could preach and help people know God. Challenge kids to be ready to live the kind of life that Jesus lived.

PRO POINTER

Choose pine cones with the petals open. You may want to let kids add seasonal silk or dried flowers around the nest. For Christmas decorations, consider using red birds and adding glitter glue to the tips of the petals.

PAPER CAPERS

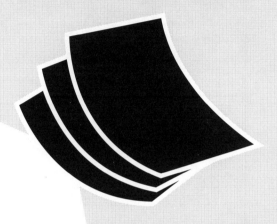

In this section, you'll need to photocopy the handouts so you have one for each child, and you'll need scissors and glue. Lead kids through the steps written on the handouts.

JUMPING FROGS

"But the people who trust the Lord will become strong again. They will rise up as an eagle in the sky; they will run and not need rest; they will walk and not become tired" (Isaiah 40:31).

Jumping frogs? Leapin' lizards! I once kept several eleven-year old boys enthralled with jumping frog contests for an entire hour at my son's birthday party.

1. Cut out the pattern on the outside line. Fold on Line A and open. Fold all four corners to Line A and open.

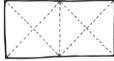

2. Turn the paper over. Fold back on Lines B and C and open. Push together the stars on Line B to form a triangle.

3. Push together the stars on Line C to form another triangle.

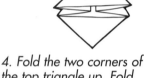

4. Fold the two corners of the top triangle up. Fold the two corners of the bottom triangle down. Now you have four legs!

5. Fold the right, left, and bottom points in toward the center and tuck them under the legs. Now you have the body!

6. Fold the bottom up at the middle line, then fold half of the bottom back. Turn your frog over. Press on the center fold line and he will jump!

84

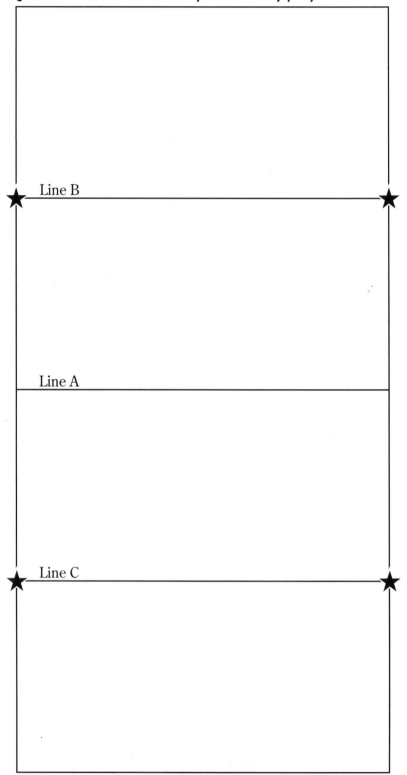

Line B

Line A

Line C

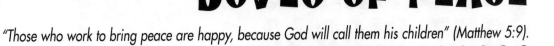

DOVES OF PEACE

"Those who work to bring peace are happy, because God will call them his children" (Matthew 5:9).

● ●

This folded, flying dove will remind children that they can be peacemakers.

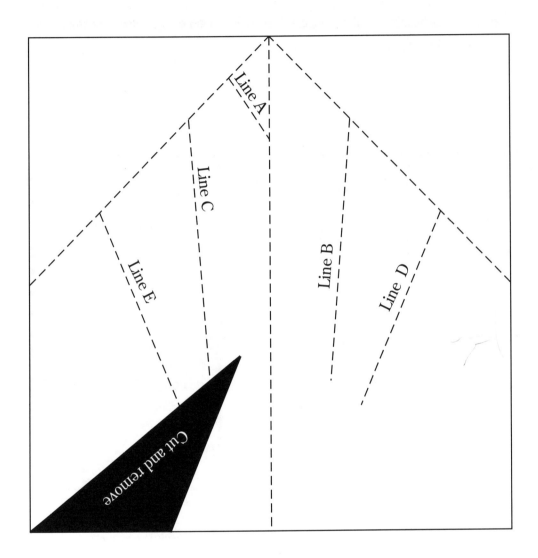

Line A

Line C

Line E

Line B

Line D

Cut and remove

1. Cut out the pattern. Fold it in half on the center dotted line, then open it, fold the top corners to the center, then fold it in half again.

2. Fold the point toward you on Line A, then fold it away from you and straighten it again. Push in on the point so the center fold reverses, forming a head.

3. Cut and remove the shaded triangle, forming a tail.

4. Fold the wings up on lines B and C. Fold the wings out on lines D and E. Your dove is ready to fly!

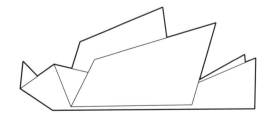

GOD'S FAMILY QUILT BLOCKS

"Jesus answered, 'Love the Lord your God with all your heart, all your soul, and with all your mind...Love your neighbor as yourself'" (Matthew 22:37, 39b).

● ● ● ● ● ● ● ● ● ● ● ● ● ● ● ● ● ● ●

Sign your name in the top left corner. In the other corners, draw or write about people and things you love. Use colored pencils to color the patterned triangles in the colors of your choice.

This colorful community-building project will show kids (and adults!) how beautiful it is to be a part of God's family.

Sign your name here.

People I love.

"Jesus answered, 'Love the Lord your God with all your heart, all your soul, and with all your mind...Love your neighbor as yourself'" (Matthew 22:37, 39b).

Places I love.

Things I love to do.

SHINING STARS

"Do everything without complaining or arguing. Then you will be innocent and without any wrong. You will be God's children without fault. But you are living with crooked and mean people all around you, among whom you shine like stars in the dark world" (Philippians 2:14-15).

● ●

This airborne art will remind kids to shine with God's love.

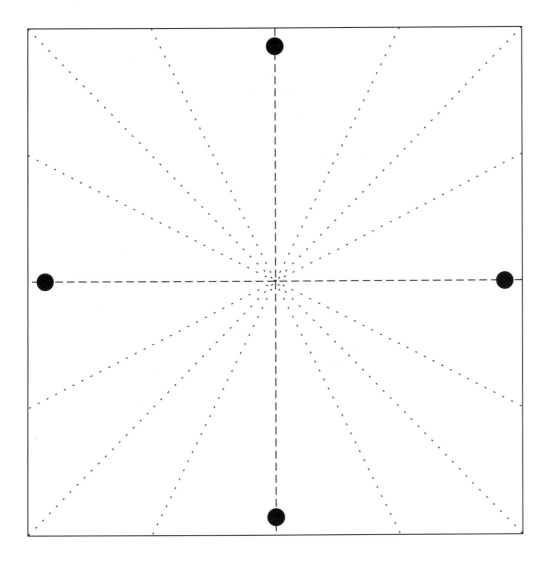

1. Cut out the pattern on the heavy lines. Use a hole punch to punch out the four circles.

2. Fold back ("valleys") on all the diagonal lines and forward ("mountains") on the cross lines.

3. Thread twenty-inch lengths of ribbon through opposite holes.

4. Pull the ribbons tight to bring the four holes together. Tie all the ribbons in a firm knot and your star is ready to fly!

PRO POINTER

For really stunning stars, cover one side of the pattern with holographic or foil wrapping paper.

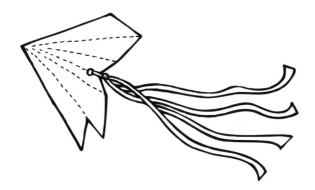

87

RiNG-A-BUCKS

"No one can serve two masters...You cannot serve both God and worldly riches" (Matthew 6:24).

● ●

Whether you use real dollar bills or play money, this craft is a ringer!

Simple George Portrait Ring

1. Fold the dollar back to make a triangle above George's head. Fold back at the bottom of the portrait—just above the "One Dollar" marking.

2. Turn the bill over. Fold the back piece from top to bottom.

3. Bring the sides behind George and slide one edge into the other.

Trickier Ring

1. Start with George upside down. Fold the bottom to the top with George inside. Note: Make all your creases very hard—run over them with a fingernail.

2. Fold in the white edges at the top and bottom and crease them hard.

3. Fold the bill in half, top to bottom, and crease it hard. The words "One Dollar" should be at the bottom.

4. Fold back on the three dotted lines as shown in the illustration.

5. To form the ring, bring the tail clockwise so it's behind the "1."

6. Unfold the "1" to the right, fold the tail up and over the ring. Fold back the white edge and tuck it into the bottom of the ring.

7. Fold the "1" to the left, fold back the white edge and tuck it into the slot made by the tail. You may need a pointed object to help you make this last tuck.

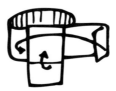

POP-UP APPRECIATION CARDS

"I have not stopped giving thanks to God for you. I always remember you in my prayers" (Ephesians 1:16).

Kids will love making 3-D pop-ups, and the happy recipients of these cards will cherish kids' thoughtfulness.

1. Cut out the card base, and fold it in half. Cut along the two solid lines of the center section and fold on the broken lines. The center fold will be a "mountain" fold, while the top and bottom folds will look like "valleys."

2. Fold the center section in so that when the card is opened, the center section pops up. Write a message on the inside of the card.

3. Cut out and decorate your favorite message design. Glue the design to the center pop-up section of the card.

4. If you wish, cover the outside of the card with construction paper or gift wrap.

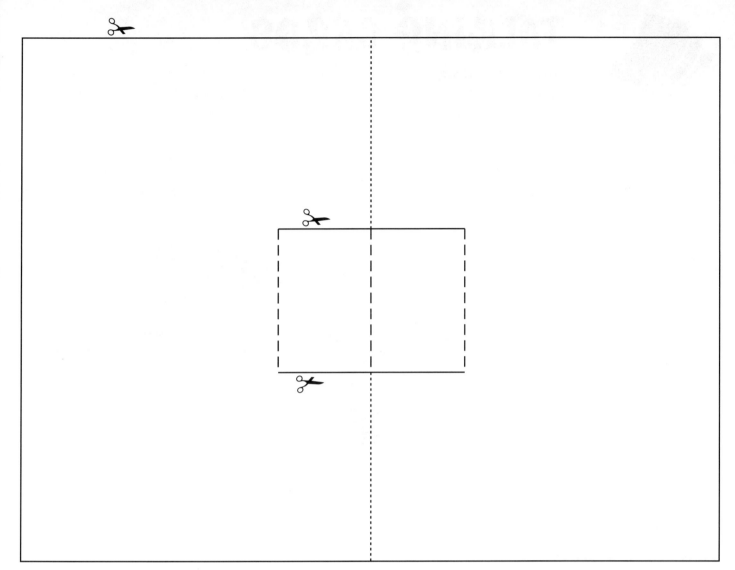

TALKING CARDS

"When you talk, do not say harmful things, but say what people need—words that will help others become stronger. Then what you say will do good to those who listen to you" (Ephesians 4:29).

● ●

These unspeakably cute cards are ready to mouth off with words of encouragement and affirmation!

1. Cut out the card on the heavy lines.

2. Fold the card in half lengthwise and cut a horizontal slit in the mouth on the solid line. Crease the mouth on the dotted lines, then unfold them.

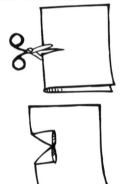

3. Open the card and reverse the center fold, so the design is on the inside. Push the mouth in toward the center fold as shown.

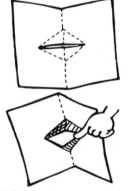

4. Write an encouraging message in the speech balloon.

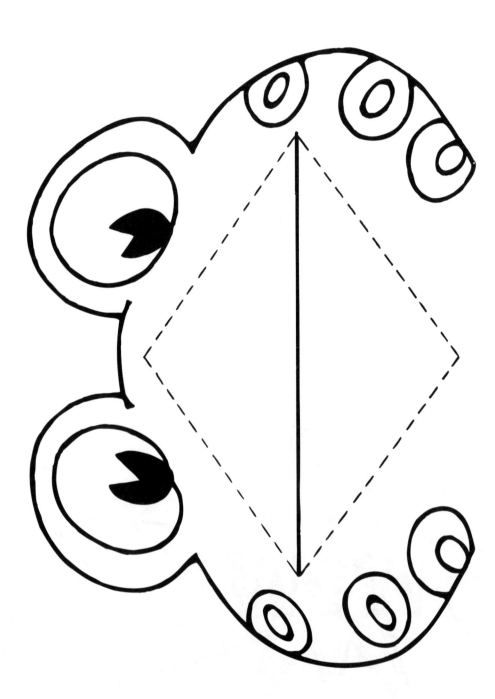

RECYCLE WRAP

"God does not see the same way people see. People look at the outside of a person, but the Lord looks at the heart" (1 Samuel 16:7b).

● ●

A great use for the good old grocery bag! This nifty idea saves money, saves trees, and makes beautiful packages.

SUPPLIES

☐ paper grocery bags
☐ scissors
☐ rubber stamps
☐ ink pads
☐ gold metallic markers

PRO POINTER

This paper looks especially nice tied with plaid ribbon or strands of raffia.

PRO POINTER

You can usually gather lots of rubber stamps by asking friends to bring what they have. Or, if you're stumped on stamps, let kids do potato prints with tempera paint.

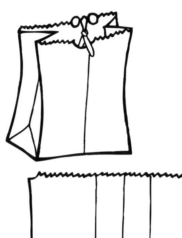

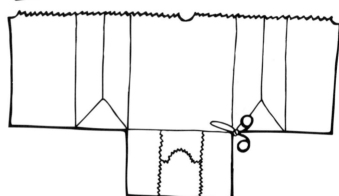

1. Demonstrate how to cut down the seam of a grocery bag, then cut away the bottom.

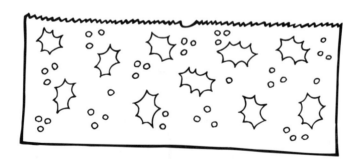

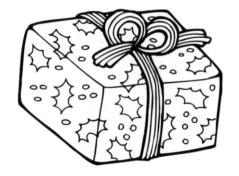

2. Flatten the paper, plain side up. Decorate it with rubber stamps and squiggles of gold metallic ink. Voilà—you have wonderful wrapping paper.

INSTANT HOLIDAY HELPERS

In this section, you'll need to photocopy the patterns so you have one for each child, and you'll need scissors, glue, and tape. Lead kids through the steps written on the handouts.

THANKSGIVING TURKEYS

Photocopy this page on yellow or orange paper. Use the turkey as a place card, or fill it with treats.

● ●

1. Lay the square with the blank side facing you. Fold in half diagonally, then open. Fold two edges to the center.

2. Turn the paper over and fold two edges to the center again.

3. Fold the larger end forward at the large square, crease, then unfold.

4. Fold back the smaller end at the large circle.

5. Fold the head forward at the dashed line. Pinch the neck in half, pull the head down, and twist the point of the head to form the turkey's wattle.

6. At the base of the neck, pull the center fold apart so the halves of the large dot touch the small dots. Pinch the base of the neck together and crease well.

7. At the other end, pull the center apart and pinch the corners so the halves of the large square touch the small squares. Crease on the dashed line.

8. Fold the corners back on the existing creases, then fold the points out again.

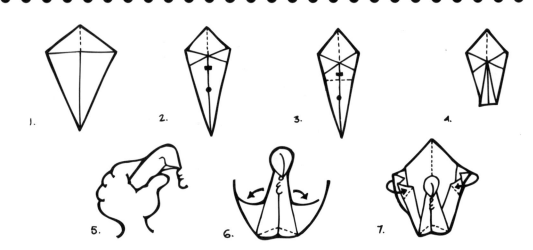

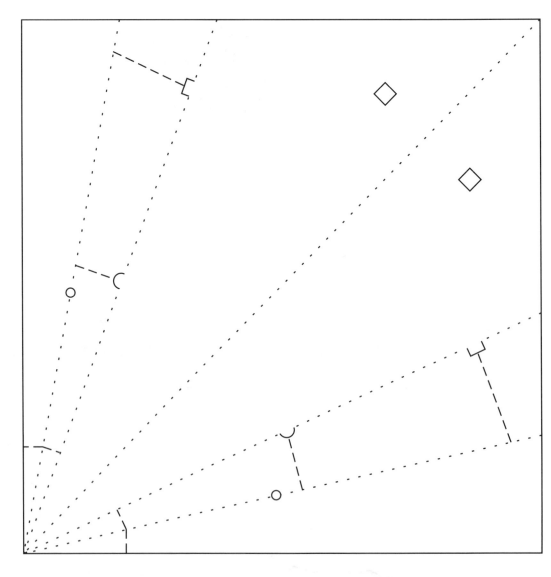

CHRISTMAS LETTER/ENVELOPES

Use this Christmas letter for invitations, Christmas greetings, or thank you notes. After you've added your message, fold in all the flaps and run a line of glue along the inside of the top flap (near the star) to seal it.

O come, let us adore him

FOLDED VALENTINE NOTES

Use these notes for Valentine sentiments or everyday messages. Write your message inside the square or on the extra heart. Fold in the side flaps, then fold in the top and bottom flaps and hook the two halves of the heart together.

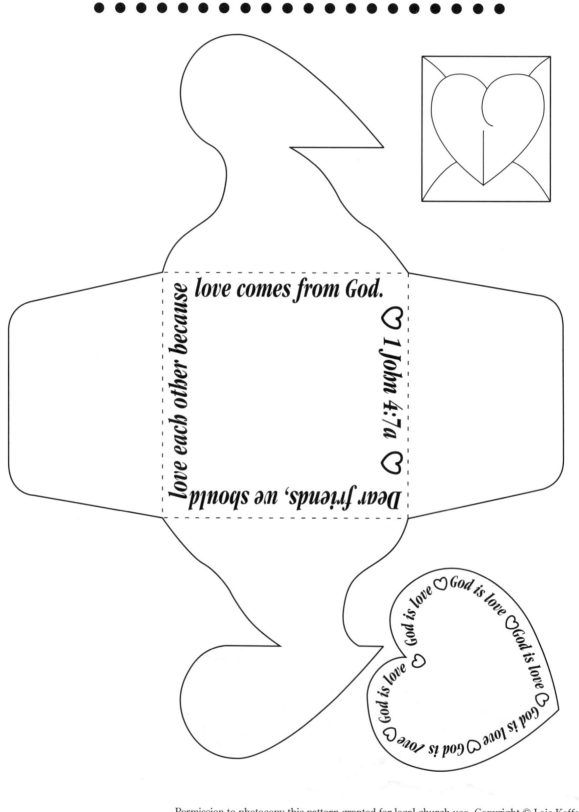

love comes from God.

love each other because

1 John 4:7a

Dear friends, we should

God is love ♡ God is love ♡ God is love ♡ God is love ♡ God is love ♡ God is love ♡ God is love ♡ God is love ♡

FOLDED EASTER BASKETS

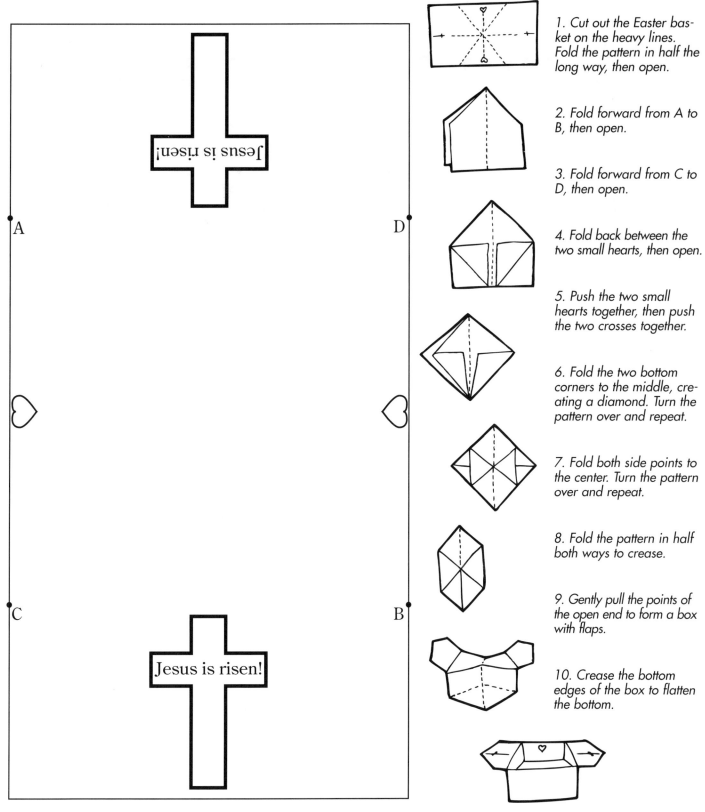

Jesus is risen! (shown upside down at top)

A   D

C   B

Jesus is risen!

1. Cut out the Easter basket on the heavy lines. Fold the pattern in half the long way, then open.

2. Fold forward from A to B, then open.

3. Fold forward from C to D, then open.

4. Fold back between the two small hearts, then open.

5. Push the two small hearts together, then push the two crosses together.

6. Fold the two bottom corners to the middle, creating a diamond. Turn the pattern over and repeat.

7. Fold both side points to the center. Turn the pattern over and repeat.

8. Fold the pattern in half both ways to crease.

9. Gently pull the points of the open end to form a box with flaps.

10. Crease the bottom edges of the box to flatten the bottom.

MOTHER'S DAY POP-UPS

Fold the card in half on the dotted line, so the top of the letters is on the crease. Cut on the heavy lines, being sure not to cut through the top of each letter. Fold up the top and bottom so the pop-up is hidden inside.

● ● ● ● ● ● ● ● ● ● ● ● ● ● ● ● ● ● ●

fold   fold

fold   fold

You're the best!

FATHER'S DAY POP-UPS

Fold the card in half on the dotted line, so the top of the letters is on the crease. Cut on the heavy lines, being sure not to cut through the top of each letter. Fold up the top and bottom so the pop-up is hidden inside.

● ●

You're the greatest!

POP-UP BIRTHDAY CAKES

Cut apart the two pieces of the card. Decorate the cake, then fold it in half and cut from A to B to C. Unfold the cake. Cut a slit on the solid, vertical line at the bottom, then fold up on the dotted line. Glue the cake to the shaded area on the other part of the card.

● ●

Glue cake here

FOLD

C

HAPPY BIRTHDAY

B

FOLD A

LUMINARIA INSTRUCTIONS

Use these instructions to assemble the luminaria on the next four pages.

• •

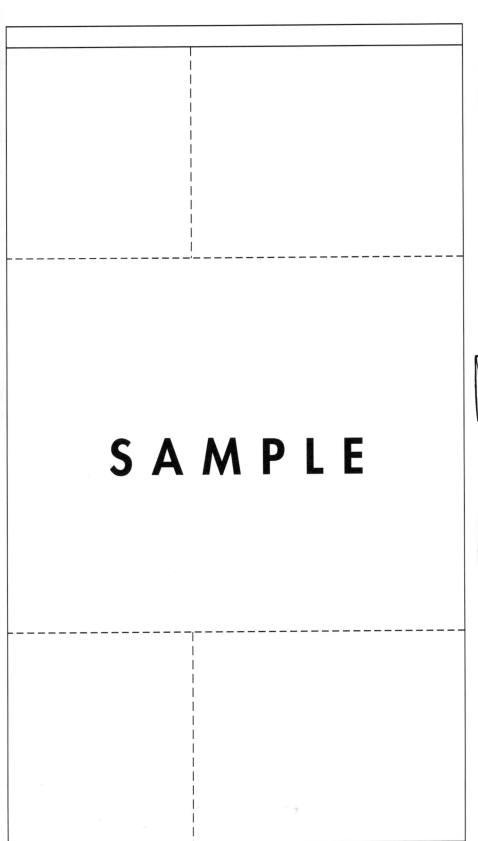

S A M P L E

1. Photocopy the handout at 150%.

2. Use a sharp pencil or pin to poke holes through the dots in the design.

3. Cut out the bag on the outside solid lines.

4. Fold the sides together and tape as shown.

Step 4

5. Fold up the bottom.

6. Push in the corners.

Step 5

7. Fold the edges in so they're even with the dotted line, then tape.

8. Pinch and crease the sides at the bottom.

Step 6

9. Place sand or pebbles in the bottom of the bag.

10. With help from an adult, place a votive candle in the center of the bag and light it.

Step 7

Step 8

THANKSGIVING LUMINARIAS

To assemble the luminaria, please follow the instructions on page 103.

GIVE THANKS

CHRISTMAS LUMINARIAS

To assemble the luminaria, please follow the instructions on page 103.

● ● ● ● ● ● ● ● ● ● ● ● ● ● ● ●

VALENTINE LUMINARIAS

To assemble the luminaria, please follow the instructions on page 103.

GOD IS LOVE

EASTER LUMINARIAS

To assemble the luminaria, please follow the instructions on page 103.

JESUS LIVES

HEART BOXES

Use this clever box for small treats and surprises. Trace the pattern onto gift wrap, then cut out the box and crease it on the dotted lines. Fold the two smaller sides in, then fold in the larger sides and connect the two halves of the heart. To make the box sturdier, cut a piece of poster board the size of the center rectangle and glue it inside the box.

● ●

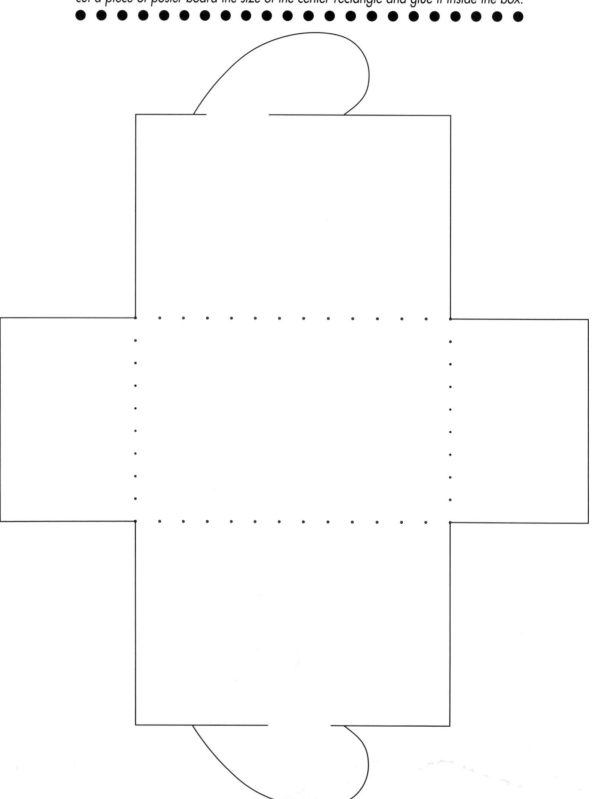

SCRIPTURE INDEX

Evaluation of
CREATIVE CAN-DO CRAFTS

Please help Group Publishing, Inc., continue to provide innovative and usable resources for ministry by taking a moment to fill out and send us this evaluation. Thanks!

● ● ●

1. As a whole, this book has been (circle one):

Not much help   Very helpful

1   2   3   4   5   6   7   8   9   10

2. The things I liked best about this book were:

3. This book could be improved by:

4. One thing I'll do differently because of this book is:

5. Optional information:

Name _____

Street Address _____

City _____ State _____ Zip _____

Phone Number _____ Date _____

BRING THE BIBLE TO LIFE FOR YOUR 1ST- THROUGH 6TH-GRADERS... WITH GROUP'S HANDS-ON BIBLE CURRICULUM™

Energize your kids with Active Learning!

Group's **Hands-On Bible Curriculum**™ will help you teach the Bible in a radical new way. It's based on active learning—the same teaching method Jesus used.

In each lesson, students will participate in exciting and memorable learning experiences using fascinating gadgets and gizmos you've not seen with any other curriculum. Your elementary students will discover biblical truths and <u>remember</u> what they learn because they're <u>doing</u> instead of just listening.

You'll save time and money too!

While students are learning more, you'll be working less—simply follow the quick and easy instructions in the **Teachers Guide**. You'll get tons of material for an energy-packed 35- to 60-minute lesson. And, if you have extra time, there's an arsenal of Bonus Ideas and Time Stuffers to keep kids occupied—and learning! Plus, you'll SAVE BIG over other curriculum programs that require you to buy expensive separate student books—all student handouts in Group's **Hands-On Bible Curriculum** are photocopiable!

In addition to the easy-to-use **Teachers Guide**, you'll get all the essential teaching materials you need in a ready-to-use **Learning Lab**®. No more running from store to store hunting for lesson materials—all the active-learning tools you need to teach 13 exciting Bible lessons to any size class are provided for you in the **Learning Lab**.

Challenging topics each quarter keep your kids coming back!

Group's **Hands-On Bible Curriculum** covers topics that matter to your kids and teaches them the Bible with integrity. Switching topics every month keeps your 1st- through 6th-graders enthused and coming back for more. The full two-year program will help your kids...

- make God-pleasing decisions,
- recognize their God-given potential, and
- seek to grow as Christians.

Take the boredom out of Sunday school, children's church, and midweek meetings for your elementary students. Make your job easier and more rewarding with no-fail lessons that are ready in a flash. Order Group's **Hands-On Bible Curriculum** for your 1st- through 6th-graders today.

Hands-On Bible Curriculum is also available for Toddlers & 2s, Preschool, and Pre-K and K!